Kessler, Carol Farley

Elizabeth Stuart Phelps

DATE DUE			

D1171356

Elizabeth Stuart Phelps

Twayne's United States Authors Series

David J. Nordloh, Editor

Indiana University, Bloomington

TUSAS 434

ELIZABETH STUART PHELPS
ca. 1880
*Photograph by Notman Photographic
Co., Ltd., Boston. Courtesy of the
Treasure Room, Haverford College
Library, Haverford, Pennsylvania.*

Elizabeth Stuart Phelps

By Carol Farley Kessler

The Pennsylvania State University
Delaware County Campus

Twayne Publishers • *Boston*

Elizabeth Stuart Phelps

Carol Farley Kessler

Copyright © 1982 by G. K. Hall & Company
All Rights Reserved
Published by Twayne Publishers
A Division of G. K. Hall & Company
70 Lincoln Street
Boston, Massachusetts   02111

Book Production by Marne B. Sultz
Book Design by Barbara Anderson

Printed on permanent/durable acid-
free paper and bound in The United
States of America.

Library of Congress Cataloging in Publication Data

Kessler, Carol Farley.
Elizabeth Stuart Phelps.

(Twayne's United States authors series;
TUSAS 434)
   Bibliography: p. 153
   Includes index.
   1. Phelps, Elizabeth Stuart, 1844–1911
—Criticism and interpretation.
I. Title. II. Series.
PS3143.K47   1982   813'.4   82-11836
ISBN 0-8057-7374-6

Contents

About the Author

Carol Farley Kessler, Assistant Professor of English and American Studies, taught from 1979–81 at the Mont Alto Campus and in 1981 joined the Delaware County Campus of the Pennsylvania State University. She specializes in composition and women's studies. She received her undergraduate training at Swarthmore College, completed an M.A.T. in English at the Harvard Graduate School of Education and her Ph.D. in American Civilization at the University of Pennsylvania. She has taught at Beaver College, Drexel University, and the University of Pennsylvania. In 1977–78 she administered a Women's Educational Equity Act (WEEA) Program at West Chester State College. She received an NEH Residential Fellowship for College Teachers to participate in a seminar meeting at the University of Maryland, 1981–82.

Professor Kessler has published several articles on Elizabeth Stuart Phelps and participated at conventions of the American Studies Association, the Modern Language Association, the National Women's Studies Association, and the Popular Culture Association. She is currently examining Utopian fiction by United States women and also pursuing a study of the lives and works of women contemporary with Phelps.

Preface

Elizabeth Stuart Phelps was a writer with a central cause—women. And because we have tended to ignore women's writing unless clearly superior in its belletristic attributes, we lost Phelps's name until the resurgence of interest in women as a subject for scholarly inquiry in the 1960s. We have, I think, found embarrassing so outspoken an advocacy for women's causes as hers was. If, however, we can accept her concern for women as a reasonable, central focus for a writing career, if we can acknowledge that writing may have other strengths worthy of our attention than the belletristic, then surely Phelps's hour "has struck," to quote her words concerning the arrival of a "Woman's Hour" in an 1879 poem for Smith College's first commencement.

I have sought to illuminate Phelps's socially innovative viewpoint. In addition, I have examined the relationship between her life and writing. Students of her work typically emphasize the extent to which her biography furnished the material for her fiction. I cannot quarrel with the emphasis. Thus I have sought to explain what psychoemotional functions her writing may have served her.

Not surprisingly, given the foregoing, this interdisciplinary study originated as a dissertation in American Civilization. Entitled "'The Woman's Hour': Life and Novels of Elizabeth Stuart Phelps, 1844-1911," the original study treated the historical value of Phelps's fiction in its depiction of women and emphasized the importance to her of a women's rights movement. My investigation demonstrated the opposing impacts upon Phelps's life and novels of a conservative Protestant socialization—which for three generations inculcated excessively anxious behavior—and a liberating women's movement that urged women, in Phelps's words, to "dream and dare." Through changing emphases in her characterizations of women Phelps revealed her own psychological needs and ambivalences. She thereby functions for us as an informant who records in her writing her responses to the living conditions experienced by women in the post-Civil-War period.

The emphasis of this current study does not differ radically from my earlier investigation. I have chosen to continue the focus upon Phelps's novels because I still consider these the most interesting segment of her work, for their revelation both of Phelps's emerging self and of women's lives in nineteenth-century New England. And they are more easily available than her scattered short fiction, much of which seems typically more moralistic than her longer fiction.

But what I consider particularly unusual and worthy of study in Phelps is the extent to which her novels mirror the psychological conditions of her life. This then is a case study in the progress of a literary woman—whose writing to be understood is inseparable from her living—from possible self-fulfillment as a writer of the first rank to disappointed alienation as the conditions of her life made the achievement of that promise impossible to her. The important factors in this progress include the influence upon her of her mother's popular fiction, her own critique of women's lives, and her insistence upon self-fulfillment as a right and possibility, given a supportive environment. Although this last aspect of her work has elicited such epithets as "sentimental," "emotional," or "wish-fulfilling," it accords with current psychotherapeutic theory.

Elizabeth Stuart Phelps thus merits attention from cultural historians and literary sociologists for her unusual position in the literary history of the United States from 1868–1911, her productive years. Hers was an international reputation, her output transcending our academic separations of "popular," "journalistic," and "belletristic" writing. Her popular "Gates" books were translated into four European languages, attesting to their appeal beyond her war-torn nation as Utopian constructions offering, especially to women, visions of more satisfying lives. Her articles on women's rights and wrongs appearing in the feminist *Woman's Journal* (est. 1870) and the *Independent* (a weekly covering literary and social matters), as well as her addresses on anti-vivisection and articles on ethical concerns, attest to her journalistic skills. And her fiction, published in the late nine-teenth century's literary pacesetters—the *Atlantic Monthly, Harper's New Monthly Magazine,* and the *Century Magazine*—demonstrates a talent at least of the second, if not the first, rank.

Upon the way to publishing my findings, I have of course incurred more debts than I can ever credit. Since I have now examined over 500 holograph letters, as well as other documents, from more than fifty institutions, let me here not list all but rather acknowledge the kind permission to publish from their holdings granted me by the American Antiquarian Society, the Andover Historical Society, the James Duncan Phillips Library of the Essex Institute, Kathi George as editor of *Frontiers: A Journal of Women Studies,* the Houghton Library of Harvard University, the Treasure Room at Haverford College, Massachusetts Historical Society, Manuscripts and Archives Division of the New York Public Library, the Arthur and Elizabeth Schlesinger Library on the History of Women in America at Radcliffe College, Friends Historical Library of Swarthmore College, Emily Toth as editor of *Regionalism and the Female Imagination,* Special Collections of Wellesley College, and the Beinecke Rare Book and Manuscript Library of Yale University. The interlibrary loan staffs at Van Pelt Library of the University of Pennsylvania and at the Mont Alto Campus of the Pennsylvania State University helped me consistently. In addition, staffs of the Rare Book Rooms of both universities contributed their expertise.

I am grateful both to the American Philosophical Society for funding research trips to several libraries (Penrose Grant No. 8040) and to the Liberal Arts College Fund for Research of the Pennsylvania State University for covering my typing expenses. For cheerful and efficient interest in the project I thank my typists Mildred Hargreaves and Jean Patrick.

For their guidance of my doctoral investigation I am indebted to committee members Elsa Greene and Gretchen Wood for substantial advice and ceaseless encouragement, and to director R. Gordon Kelly for unerring good judgment and the freedom to pursue self-defined goals. Since then several colleagues have read and commented upon part or all of the work. Cathy N. Davidson,

Michigan State University, commented upon my analysis of the mother-daughter aspect of Phelps's work, while Emily Toth of Pennsylvania State University reviewed the studies of Phelps's view on marriage and use of humor. Most recently, Judith Fetterley, the State University of New York at Albany, reviewed the doctoral investigation as a whole and made valuable suggestions for the present study. Finally, I appreciate the helpful suggestions from editors at G. K. Hall. And three generations of my family—parent, spouse, and children—have cooperated generously in providing the support that freed me to complete this work. To all the foregoing I offer my thanks for both their comments and their belief in the work. Any errors remaining are my own.

Carol Farley Kessler

The Pennsylvania State University
Delaware County Campus

Chronology

1844   August 31, Mary Gray, first child, born in Boston to the Reverend Austin Phelps and Elizabeth Wooster Stuart.

1848   Family moves to Andover, where father joins the faculty of the Andover Theological Seminary.

1849   M[oses] Stuart Phelps, a brother, born.

1851   *The Sunny Side*, mother's popular book.

1852   Deaths of grandfather Moses Stuart and mother; birth of brother A[mos] Lawrence Phelps. Probably assumes mother's name.

1854   Father's marriage to aunt, Mary Stuart, then tubercular.

1855   Death of maternal grandmother.

1856   Death of Mary Stuart Phelps.

1858   Father's marriage to Mary Ann Johnson.

1860   Reads *Aurora Leigh*; birth of brother Francis Johnson Phelps; completes Mrs. Edwards' School for Young Ladies.

1863   Edward Johnson Phelps ("Trotty") born.

1864   Begins *The Gates Ajar*; publishes first *Tiny* book.

1865   *Up Hill. Mercy Gliddon's Work.*

1866   *Tiny.* "Jane Gurley's Story." Three *Gypsy* books.

1867   Fourth *Gypsy* book. Last two *Tiny* books.

1868   *The Gates Ajar.*

1869   *Men, Women, and Ghosts* (short fiction).

1870   *Hedged In. The Trotty Book.*

1871   *The Silent Partner.* The *Woman's Journal* and *Independent* articles on women's issues; ill health.

1872   "Our Little Woman."

1873   *Trotty's Wedding Tour, and Story-book. What to Wear?* "Hannah Colby's Chance."

1874   Rebuts Dr. E. H. Clarke on women's health.

1875   *Poetic Studies.* Establishes Gloucester Temperance Reform Club.

1876   George Eliot lectures at Boston University. Builds Gloucester cottage.

1877   *The Story of Avis.* Ill health.

1878   Austin Phelps's essay against woman suffrage.

1879   *Old Maid's Paradise. Sealed Orders* (short fiction). *My Cousin and I* (London).

1881   *Friends: A Duet.* Austin Phelps's essay against woman suffrage.

1882   *Doctor Zay.*

1883   Death of brother Stuart Phelps. *Beyond the Gates.* "A Brave Girl."

1885   *Songs of the Silent World and Other Poems.*

1886   Death of friend Dr. Mary Briggs Harris. *Burglars in Paradise. The Madonna of the Tubs.*

1887   *The Gates Between. Jack the Fisherman.* Ill health.

1888   Marriage to Herbert Dickinson Ward.

1889   *The Struggle for Immortality* (essays).

1890   *The Master of the Magicians* (with H. D. Ward). Death of father. Joins First Baptist Church in Newton.

1891   *Austin Phelps: A Memoir. A Last Hero* and *Come Forth*, each with H. D. Ward. *Fourteen to One* (short fiction).

1893   Newton home built. *Donald Marcy.*

1895   *A Singular Life.*

1896   *Chapters from a Life.* Begins anti-vivisection interest. *The Supply at St. Agatha's.*

1897   *The Story of Jesus Christ: An Interpretation.*

1899 *Loveliness: A Story.*

1901 *The Successors of Mary the First. Within the Gates.* Anti-vivisection addresses before committee of Massachusetts Legislature.

1902 *Avery. Confessions of a Wife.* Anti-vivisection address.

1904 *Trixy.* Third anti-vivisection address.

1906 *The Man in the Case.*

1907 *Walled In: A Novel.*

1908 *Though Life Us Do Part. The Whole Family,* by twelve authors.

1909 *Jonathan and David. The Oath of Allegiance and Other Stories.*

1910 *A Chariot of Fire. The Empty House and Other Stories.*

1911 January 28, dies in Newton home. *Comrades.*

Chapter One
Of Ancestry and Childhood

Elizabeth Stuart Phelps was born August 31, 1844, in the parsonage of the Pine Street Congregational Church at 99 Harrison Avenue, Boston. She was named "Mary Gray Phelps" for an intimate friend of her mother. Phelps claimed in her autobiography, *Chapters from a Life* (1896), that hers was a literary life beginning long before she was actually born. She came from a line of doctrine-writing clergymen and fiction-writing women. Her family's New England roots extended back to 1650 on the maternal side and to 1630 on the paternal. Her grandfathers on both sides were Calvinist divines and her grandmothers thus ministers' dutiful wives. Her mother's generation added the duties of writer to those of minister's wife. This combination of minister and wife seems to have created patterns of dysfunctional behavior in each of the three generations mentioned. In addition, Phelps would note in the 1896 autobiography, "The grandfather who belonged to the underground-railway [paternal], and the grandfather of the German lexicon [maternal], must have contended in the brain cells or heart cells of their unconscious descendent, as our ancestors do in the lives of all of us; for the reformer's blood and the student's blood have always had an uncomfortable time of it, together in my veins."[1]

Both Stuart and Phelps men held what granddaughter Phelps would call a "feudal" view of women. She explained—

Andover was a heavily masculine place.... At the subject of eminent women the Hill had not yet arrived. I have sometimes wondered what would have been the fate even of my mother, had she lived to work her power to its bloom.... The best of [Andover's] good men were too feudal in their views of women in those days, to understand [an eminent woman's] life.... We have moved on since then, so fast and so far, that it is almost as hard now for us to understand the perplexity with which intelligent, even instructed men, used to consider the phenomenon of a superior woman, as it was then for such men to understand such a woman at all. (*Chapters*, 133-34)

The "Feudal View": Stuart Version

Her maternal grandfather, the Reverend Moses Stuart (1780-1852), was minister of a Congregational church in New Haven from 1806 to 1810, when he accepted a professorship of Greek and Hebrew literature at Andover [Massachusetts] Theological Seminary. There, by his introduction of German historical criticism, he revolutionized American biblical studies. He wrote several scholarly works concerning Hebrew grammar and the new German criticism. He appears to have gained his eminence at the price of imposing a rigid and exacting life upon his family as well as upon himself. His eldest daughter Elizabeth Wooster Stuart Phelps (1815-1852)—who would become Elizabeth Phelps's mother—retained childhood memories of his self-discipline and sleeplessness, and of the high standards that he set for his children's work.

Another daughter, Sarah Stuart Robbins (1817-1910)—Phelps's maternal aunt and eventual neighbor—detailed her father's inflexibly observed daily routine. Meals were served punctually with all family members present, illness alone permitting their absence. Moses's own activities of study, reading, and outdoor exercise likewise followed a schedule. Even friends' request that he perform a 10 A.M. marriage ceremony could not move him to relax his "absolute law." By 9:00 P.M. all must be quiet for a "diseased nervous system and an overtaxed brain"; even so, Moses glided about the house seeking sleep but finding none. Still, he was "a most generous father—when he remembered...."[2]

The burdens of maintaining so rigid a routine in a household of several lively children fell upon Moses's wife (Phelps's maternal grandmother), Abigail Clark Stuart (1783-1855). She did, however, enjoy the help of several domestic servants, whose management was of course her responsibility. Although an invalid, believed for many years to be near death, Abigail successfully accomplished such household management: she kept before her children the belief that their father was "chosen and set apart from the rest of the world to do a great and important work." And never, wrote Sarah, did her mother speak ill of any person. Upon Abigail's death in 1855, her neighbor Harriet Beecher Stowe (1811–1896) could write, "of life's long sickness healed, / A saint hath risen, where pain no more may come": she had completed her "patient mother's hourly martyrdom." In Stowe's view, Abigail represented an ideal woman rewarded by heavenly sainthood for her earthly sacrifices.[3]

Human beings, however, become ideals—mere social constructs—at a price. The nervous sleeplessness of Moses Stuart and the invalidism of Abigail Stuart, coupled with a rigidly regulated daily routine, suggest that both may have suffered unrecognized inner tensions, repressed in order to maintain what they apparently both accepted as properly managed lives. Two possible explanations for their symptoms—which constituted a pattern to be repeated in two generations following them—are nineteenth-century moral philosophy and twentieth-century psychology of neurosis. The latter suggests how the former may have created irreconcilable tensions, as individual lives collided with cultural expectations.[4]

Intellectual historian Donald H. Meyer has found that courses in moral philosohy, required of the nation's college-educated men born before 1860, helped to form America's public conscience. Men thus educated guided their wives and daughters in developing a sense of Christian duty as taught by such courses. Oberlin's President Asa Mahan (1799–1889) argued that "a full and *perfect* discharge of our entire duty.... implies the *entire* absence of *all* selfishness, and the *perpetual* presence and all pervading influence of pure and *perfect* love" (italics mine).[5] An individual's moral progress was indicated by accurate judgment of morality and a capacity always to act in accord with a sense of duty. The inability to meet so great an expectation would likely have created within such individuals tension between what they believed they "ought to be"—an idealized self-image—and what they saw themselves as being—persons falling short of this ideal.

The twentieth-century psychoanalyst Karen Horney has used the term "neurotic" for people who try to protect the conscious self against such inner tension. Horney theorizes that a neurotic gives the "major part of his energies to the task of molding himself, by a rigid system of inner dictates, into a being of absolute perfection.... able to endure anything, to understand everything, to like everybody, to be always productive." Horney calls these inner dictates "the tyranny of the should."[6] The similarity between Horney's "tyranny of the should" and Meyer's representation of the academic moralists' "sense of duty" is striking. In fact, a third researcher—Bernard J. Paris, in his use of Horney's theory to analyze nineteenth-century fiction—has found that, like moral philosophy, much of that fiction also justifies the neurotic solution of shaping the self into an idealized image.[7] The "tyranny of the should" leads a person to make not only exaggerated claims upon the self, but also excessive demands upon others—for example, Moses Stuart's expecting his wife to manage the household according to his own standards of professional practice. His exacting standards permitted him both to insist that others as well live up to those standards and then to despise them for failing also. He thus externalized his own self-condemnation. Such insomnia as he experienced is among the symptoms of inner tension that Horney describes.

Abigail Stuart's invalidism can be interpreted as her response to Moses Stuart's excessive expectations for her. She apparently responded to her wifely duty of submission by effacing herself in a life dedicated to husband and family. Her daughter Sarah and her neighbor Harriet Beecher Stowe viewed Abigail as an exemplar of perfect, loving devotion. A family system in which the neurotic needs of one member create neurotic responses in another was thus established. But although such compliance seems humanitarian and supportive of family welfare, it can destroy an individual's emotional well-being by requiring that she overlook her own needs. In company with other nineteenth-century women, Abigail could have found relief from flawless household management by assuming the socially acceptable role of sickness or invalidism (a term used at the time to mean "ill health"). The lives of both her daughter and granddaughter would exhibit similar patterns.

In addition to burdens placed upon wives and mothers, other instances of the subordination of Andover women existed. For one example, Sarah Stuart Robbins noted that at schooltime the boys walked along a broad, graveled walk to a tall brick building, the girls along a narrow footpath to a little brown schoolhouse, "a comparison not wholly agreeable to [the latter's] self-esteem." As another example, Sarah reported, "little girls or grown women, we were never legitimate parts of this Andover life [of week-day meetings]. . . . We joined in the prayers in the half-hearted manner of those who feel themselves outsiders." And yet in spite of such second-class status, the very establishment of Andover Theological Seminary had been made possible in 1808 by a woman, Mme Phoebe Phillips, who had contributed to its facilities her own property. In addition to such philanthropy, women might also write or teach. But Andover's female half was viewed as subordinate, and certainly its achievements went largely unacknowledged. Two generations of Stuart women could not have missed being aware of their limited place in Andover affairs.[8]

A remarkable woman to emerge from such an environment was Elizabeth Wooster Stuart Phelps, the mother of "Mary Gray Phelps." For a few years she combined a successful career as writer with her domestic responsibilities of managing a minister's household and children. She was born in Andover, August 13, 1815, the Stuarts' second daughter. At birth she joined three brothers, the oldest of whom was six. She was believed to resemble her father both in appearance and intellectuality. Even as a child of ten, she showed her talent by composing extemporaneous stories to amuse family domestics and their friends as well as her younger sisters. But offsetting such positive traits as her narrative skill and appreciation for painting, sculpture, and music, was a deep fear lest her mother die. The mother's invalid state left the daughter in the care of a nurse, whose entertainment consisted of attending village funerals accompanied by her small charge. This experience, her husband believed, led her as an adult to write "sunny" Sunday school stories illustrating religious principle "as it is in life" rather than repeating the typical formula of early piety anticipating early death.[9]

Educated at Abbot Academy, Phelps's mother at sixteen went to Boston, where she attended the Mount Vernon School and lived for two years in the family of the Reverend Jacob Abbott (1803–1879), author of the Rollo stories for children. While there, her first published work—brief articles written over the name "H. Trusta," an anagram of Stuart—appeared in a religious magazine edited by Abbott. Her father's approval of this work meant more to her than that of 400,000 readers of her later work. The effort to obtain parental approval, as well as her efforts in "bringing to perfection the nature [God had given her]," left Phelps's mother feeling so inadequate and lacking in self-confidence that at the end of her life she complained, "I have struggled hard to know my duty in life, and to do it. I do not feel as if I had succeeded, but nobody knows how I have struggled to do right." The pattern would be repeated in the relationship of *her* daughter to her own father (Elizabeth Stuart's husband).[10]

In the spring of 1834 Phelps's mother returned to Andover because she suffered from "cerebral disease," believed to have been caused by overexertion at school; her daughter would instead attribute the illness to the lack of intellectual stimulation.[11] For three or four years afterwards, Phelps's mother experienced severe and frequent headaches, partial blindness, temporary paralysis of portions of her body, and great prostration of the nervous system. Her family believed such physical suffering naturally preceded the religious conversion that culminated in her becoming, in July, 1834, the first Stuart child to join the chapel of the Andover Theological Seminary. Her physical condition after conversion, however, worsened to such a degree in an attack of typhus fever that death was feared. Of this period, Phelps's mother wrote: "Suppressed longings, and unsatisfied tastes, and despised capacities, at length took their revenge. They fretted, and chafed, and wore upon the delicate frame-work that enclosed them, until it gave way. Then followed four long, dreary years." But, she continued, "from the very first half hour in which I broke down the barriers of my old system, and took up my pencil, I said, 'Good bye to doctors.'" In fact, it appears that religious self-denial had aggravated her health and that her daughter's interpretation of the ill health was more likely than her family's. By about 1838 she had improved, but never fully recovered.[12]

Such an array of symptoms as Phelps's mother exhibited suggests severe internal stress—the breakdown of defenses established to maintain the self before impossible standards. Helen Sootin Smith has interpreted Phelps family illnesses as a "culturally sanctioned way of dealing with repression."[13] The symptoms also suggest the so-called "hysterical women" studied by the historian Carroll Smith-Rosenberg, who believes that hysteria was a "social role produced by and functional within a specific set of social circumstances." She notes,

At a time when American society accepted egalitarian democracy and free will as transcendent social values, women...were nevertheless routinely socialized to fill a weak, dependent and severely limited social role.... The effect of this socialization was to teach women to have a low evaluation of themselves, to significantly restrict their ego functions to low prestige areas, to depend on others and to altruistically wish not for their own worldly success, but for that of their male supporters.

Thus it appears that upon various cultural levels from the national to the individual, the symptoms that Phelps's mother experienced were in Smith-Rosenberg's words "both product and indictment of her culture."[14]

The Stuart household, in spite of so sombre an atmosphere, had its lighter moments, too. The daughter Elizabeth Stuart Phelps reported that the Stuart children knew how to have a good time and that the four daughters (one being her mother) were the "sirens of Andover Hill," who provided "justifiable recreation" for theological students. She characterized her mother as having been "grave" and "vivacious" at this time. And so it was not surprising that a comparably "grave" student, Austin Phelps (1820–1890), would, in September, 1842, marry her.[15]

The Feudal View: Phelps Version

Whereas in the Stuart view a woman was to be subsumed by a man, in the Phelps version she was to be idolized by him. Austin's father (thus Phelps's paternal grandfather), the Reverend Eliakim Phelps (1789–1880) prided himself that every male bearer of the family name was "either a minister or dignitary of the Church of Christ." Between 1814, after Eliakim had graduated from Union College, and 1816, when he was called to his first pastorate in West Brookfield, Massachusetts, he had read theology with a pastor of Wilbraham, Massachusetts, where in the choir of the village church sang a "young and beautiful one . . . waiting for his coming," Sarah Adams (1793–1845), whom he must have married about 1816. Of her (Phelps's paternal grandmother), he reportedly said in his old age, "Nine and twenty years we walked together, and I never knew her to do a wrong thing, or to say an unwise one." His "never" indicates both his acceptance of the then-conventional ideal of womanly perfection and his belief that his wife had adequately fulfilled the ideal. Whether or not Eliakim's statement about his wife accurately renders her behavior, his expectation of her perfection must always have been before her as the impossible goal toward which she must tune her being. His granddaughter affirmed that he had never viewed his wife "apart from the conventional ideal of his times" (*A. Phelps*, 10). His son Austin observed that he was "one of the many successful pastors who owe their success largely to prudent and godly wives," and added that his father was one of the few who "have the grace to see and acknowledge the obligation."[16]

Austin's sense that his father's success was owing to his mother indicates his belief that many men by themselves could not achieve success, that a man required a wife to make his success possible. In fact, he was right: to fulfill such professional demands, a man did not have time to meet his own housekeeping needs. An assumed division of labor by sex did facilitate his professional success. The sociologist Philip Slater refers in addition to an "emotional division of labor" whereby husbands "use their wives as opiates to soften the impact" of daily pressure.[17] Thus the conventional woman-worship of a husband and son must be seen merely as the brighter side of a shaded coin. The shaded side was of course the marital and maternal responsibilities that could become so burdensome as to prevent a woman's comparable success in a career.

Unlike Moses Stuart, Eliakim Phelps was a revivalist preacher, compared by his son to Oberlin's tempestuous Charles Grandison Finney (1792–1875). Among the clergy, Eliakim was the first in the country to establish a Sunday school and the first in Worcester County, Massachusetts, to remove liquor from his sideboard. Although upon assuming his first pastorate in West Brookfield he had quickly effected a revival, he was disappointed that a second did not occur during his ten-year ministry. He therefore resigned in 1826 to accept the principalship of Young Ladies' High School (later Maplewood School) in Pittsfield, Massachusetts. But as this did not suit him, he accepted a local pastorate and again caused a revival.

By 1830 he was settled as pastor in Geneva, New York, where he remained six years. He seems to have preached in towns and cities throughout upstate New York to the extent that his young son Austin judged life to be a continuous revival. His father reputedly converted around two thousand. In addition, he aided slaves escaping north along the Underground Railroad if they passed by his door, but refused to take a vocal part in abolitionist activity "because he revered the Scriptures and the Church of Christ more than he did anybody's civil freedom."[18]

The Geneva years were ended by an attack of cholera, which permanently damaged Eliakim's health and left him unable to undertake the labors of a settled pastor. Consequently, he accepted secretaryships of the American Education Society, first in Philadelphia and then in New York, positions he held until retirement. During this last period, while residing in his Stratford, Connecticut, parsonage, Eliakim experienced, beginning in March, 1850, what he considered a seven-month spiritualist visitation—but more likely the ingenious tricks of his younger son. His religious tract recording these events reached a circulation of 200,000 copies. Eliakim's interest in Sunday schools, practice of temperance, concern for humanity, and spiritualist experience would find expression again in the life and work of his granddaughter.

Eliakim Phelps's life seems to have been one of restless questing after external self-validation: he required ever another revival to demonstrate his human worth. When a second revival did not occur, he left; when principalship did not fit his needs, he raised another revival, surely an event likely both to make him feel all-powerful—a veritable deputy of Omnipotence—and to give him the illusion that his self-glorification was reality.

On January 10, 1820, in Brookfield, Massachusetts, Phelps's father, Austin—a first son and second child—was born to Sarah and Eliakim; a sister who would survive only twelve years was then three. Austin reportedly was a precocious child, who at four read the Bible and at eight worked cube roots. No child, however, learns such skills without adult involvement. Given his intense and lifelong self-doubt, Austin may have been made to feel that no achievement was good enough. His reported childhood flawlessness suggests that anything less would have been unacceptable.

In addition to self-doubt, like his wife-to-be Austin developed a morbid horror of death; he was compelled to attend funerals, a fate he occasionally managed to escape by clever hiding. The household's frequent moves must also have increased his insecurity. His peripatetic father of course moved his family with each change of his own position. First Austin was schooled in Dr. Dewey's School, Pittsfield, from 1828–1829. Then his sister died during the one year that he attended Wilbraham Academy. When his father moved to Geneva, Austin himself experienced a revival of religion—a feverish, unsettling experience.

At the age of thirteen Austin entered Hobart College in Geneva, New York, and continued two years. Then he spent six months at Amherst College. For a lad fraught with self-doubt, association with students more mature than he must have aggravated already strong anxiety: "too early he left [his mother]," his daughter noted (*A. Phelps*, 27-29). In 1835, upon entering the University of Pennsylvania, he finally rejoined his peers and was graduated as valedictorian of the Class of 1837. Owing to his failure to have the conversion experience that he desired and expected, his eighteenth year was agonizing and unsuccessful. Referring to this experience, Austin expressed his aversion to Christian emotional ecstasy; rather, he felt obedience to an earthly father the appropriate medium of regeneration.

In preparation for the clergy he studied Hebrew at New York [Union] Seminary, and in 1839 attended the New Haven [Yale] Seminary. In 1840 he was licensed to preach by the Third Presbytery of Philadelphia and delivered his first sermon in the Old Arch Street Church. But, still feeling unready for clerical responsibilities (one of his continual expressions of self-doubt), he pursued further study at Andover, where he was a resident licentiate listed under the Class of 1842. There he met at the home of Moses Stuart the eldest daughter. In 1842 he accepted the call of the Pine Street Church, Boston, upon their second invitation, and was ordained in April, 1842. In September of the same year, Austin married Elizabeth Stuart; they settled into the Harrison Avenue parsonage, where their daughter was born and where they remained six years.

Austin expressed acute dissatisfaction with his pastorate. He saw himself as having lacked self-trust and thus having found no repose in his work. He considered none of the three hundred sermons written during this period worth saving, and yet his performance was such that the Andover faculty called him to the Chair of Rhetoric. Intense self-doubt in the face of public approbation seemed to plague Austin all of his life. He seemed never to feel adequate to the job at hand even though his contemporaries found much in his work to praise. His self-minimizing surely reached abnormal heights: letters written throughout his life show him unable to recognize redeeming virtues in himself. A revealing passage occurs in a letter of June 10, 1876, to his sister-in-law, Sarah Stuart Robbins (Phelps's maternal aunt): "To me the day of judgment seems more valuable for its righting the self accusations of good people, than for its condemnation of the wicked.... These awful tribunals of Conscience need an illuminating from infinite Love, and they are sure to get it" (*A. Phelps*, 235).

Upon his election to the Andover faculty, he waited for two months before reluctantly agreeing to relinquish the pulpit, a position which he had believed to be his lifeblood—"an inheritance from his honored father," to be valued over any professorship (*A. Phelps*, 40). He accepted the Andover call only because he believed the Chair would be less of a physical drain than the pulpit upon a constitution whose breakdown he believed close at hand. In fact, such a breakdown did occur upon his arrival in Andover: Phelps developed a case of amaurosis and was unable to assume his professorial duties for some months. So intensely expected a breakdown, providing an acceptable excuse for withdrawal, offers an attractive solution in freeing the sufferer from the self-accusation that failure to meet his own standard of perfection would have brought.

Phelps's mother was comparably lacking in optimism regarding the call to Andover, since she believed the Boston years the "happiest...of her life." She especially dreaded the breaking up through death of her father's family and having to live in Andover with "only their graves to visit"; she "concealed in great measure the foreboding with which she anticipated the change, lest [her husband's] decision be unduly influenced by a knowledge of her feelings." Unfortunately for both, social practice decreed that a man make a career decision largely upon its merit, and pay insufficient regard to its effect upon the emotional tone of his household. His wife's compliance in this practice was self-destructive, exposing her once again to what for her was an inhospitable environment. Her self-effacing posture, learned in accommodating her father, now kept her from asserting her own needs: she should be content with little.[19]

Andover Childhood

Their daughter "Mary Gray" was nearly four when the Phelpses moved to Andover in 1848. Within the year she was joined by a brother, Moses Stuart, born in March, 1849, and called "Stuart." Recalling her mother, Phelps wrote: "My first distinct vision... gives her by the nursery lamp, reading to us her own stories, written for ourselves, never meant to go beyond that little public of two, and illustrated in colored crayons by her own pencil. For her gift in this direction was of an original quality, and had she not been a writer she must have achieved something as an artist" (*Chapters*, 13).

One group of such stories was posthumously published, *Little Mary; or Talks and Tales for Children* (1854). Her husband noted that her children's needs stimulated her to write stories for them: the chapters concern Mary's learning new words, new behavior, new information as she grows from five to seven to nine. A mother who writes and a father who instructs his daughter figure prominently in the tales. Especially interesting is Mary's mother's promise to write her a new book to be composed of story-presents for May-day, birthday, and Christmas. Mary, who thought "great people" wrote books, discovers that her own mother is among them.[20] Although we cannot assume that the content of this volume exactly reports the facts of young Phelps's life, we do learn what her mother believed appropriate behavior for a growing girl—that she persevere, be orderly, accomplish her work, accommodate others, accept what could not be helped; that her good behavior would be rewarded by a fishing party, a carriage ride, a row on the river; that her parents had reasons for their requests and thereby helped their daughter to rationalize her childish world. In sum, the stories show the mother setting the standards and the father rewarding their being well-met.

During the scant five years that Phelps's mother resided again in Andover, she strove "till she fell" (*Chapters*, 15). In her daughter's words, "a wife, a mother, a housekeeper, a hostess, in delicate health, on an academic salary, undertakes a deadly load when she starts upon a literary career" (*A. Phelps*, 87). Particularly when she had a "silent determination to achieve a supreme result," she may succeed in making a man "divinely happy. But she may die in trying to do so" (*A. Phelps*, 53).

She had lived thirty years before she made a career of her writing, experiencing a long silence before beginning to write, a pattern especially typical of women.[21] Even so, her realistic portrayals of the wives of New England clergymen were instantly popular. Originally written as a portrait of a deceased friend (Mary Gray?), *The Sunny Side; or, a Country Minister's Wife* (1851) sold 100,000 copies during its first year.[22] *A Peep at "Number Five": or, A Chapter in the Life of a City Pastor* (1852), which derived from her own experience and which she favored as "her best effort," sold 20,000 in less than a year.[23] In addition, there was the "Kitty Brown" series for the American Sunday School Union and two collections of adult magazine fiction. Especially revealing is the story *Angel over the Right Shoulder* (1852). Through the principal character, Mrs. James, Phelps's mother dwelt upon her own concerns:

She thought of her disappointment and the failure of her plans. To her, not only the past month but the whole year, seemed to have been one of fruitless effort—all broken and disjointed—even her hours of religious duty had been encroached upon, and disturbed. She had accomplished nothing, that she could see, but to keep her house and family in order, and even this, to her saddened mind, seemed to have been but indifferently done. She was conscious of yearnings for a more earnest life than this. Unsatisfied longings for something which she had not attained, often clouded what, otherwise, would have been a bright day to her; and yet the causes of these feelings seemed to lie in a dim and misty region, which her eye could not penetrate.

What then did she need? To see *results* from her life's work? To know that a golden cord bound her life-threads together into *unity* of purpose—notwithstanding they seemed, so often, single and broken?

She was quite sure that she felt no desire to shrink from duty, however humble, but she sighed for some comforting assurance of what *was duty.* Her employments, conflicting as they did with her tastes, seemed to her frivolous and useless. It seemed to her that there was some better way of living, which she, from deficiency in energy of character, or of principle, had failed to discover.[24]

Mrs. James then dreams of two angels, one over each shoulder.[25] The angel over her left shoulder records with disapproval the self-concern distracting her from her home and children, while the angel over her right shoulder "required of her no great deeds, but faithfulness and patience to the end of the race which was set before her. Now she could see plainly enough, that though it was right and important for her to cultivate her own mind and heart, it was equally right and equally important, to meet and perform faithfully all those little household cares and duties on which the comfort of her family depended" (37). Although Mr. James appears well-intentioned in urging his wife to devote time to her own interests, he lacks awareness of his own intrusions upon her life. Since Phelps's mother's life too was difficult, she invented a dream in which she imagined angels *over* a woman's shoulders recognizing her efforts as no one else did. Phelps, writing of her parents' relationship, noted that her father took a "feudal view of lines of feeling and action which should be found natural to women," that he never looked beyond her "fireside graces" (*A. Phelps*, 87).

One year before her death, Phelps's mother wrote in her "Family Journal" that *Sunny Side*

has succeeded ... beyond my most sanguine dreams. It appears to me that the way is now opening for me to write,—a way which I have sighed for, long. I do pray that my fondness for it may not lead me to overrate my ability for it, or its comparative importance. At present, I do not understand either what I can, or precisely what I wish to do in this way. I work in the dark. Everything lies in chaos before me. My life is a riddle to me; the past is all I can read. *I cannot tell a letter* of the future.[26]

Unfortunately for all concerned, little future remained. Her son Stuart's illness sapped her energies. Before she could recover, her father died in January, 1852—"an event which shocked her whole system" because "the cord that had so long bound her life to his, would not break": she could not accept his death.[27] She found relief in redoubled exertions to write as she composed and revised *A Peep at "Number Five."* Pregnant throughout these events with her third child—Amos Lawrence, who was born in August, 1852,—she herself died November 29. "Her last book and her last baby came together and killed her," the daugher believed

(*Chapters*, 12). In accordance with the mother's dying wish, her infant was baptized beside her coffin as part of her funeral. Two other wishes were less scrupulously observed—that her daughter be trained in the fine arts and her two sons for the foreign missions.

The mother's influence did not end with death. After completing her early schooling at Abbot Academy, the daughter entered Mrs. Edwards' School for Young Ladies; she was by then proudly known by her mother's name, Elizabeth Stuart Phelps. Exactly when the change occurred or by whose initiative is not entirely clear. Most sources assert that Phelps at her mother's death chose to be called by her mother's name.[28] Of greater concern is the symbolic force that using her mother's name would have had. Early in life the ego boundary between mother and daughter nominally disappeared: one name identified both. Her choice of career indicates the strength of this identification.

Gains and losses succeeded each other during the next few years. In 1854 her father married her aunt Mary Stuart (1822–1856), then suffering from tuberculosis. Phelps believed her father married his sister-in-law partly out of a heavy sense of responsibility, in order that he might nurse her. Like her three sisters, the second mother also wrote: she translated many German works, for a woman at that time a rare achievement. And a year and a half later, this mother, devoted to her sister's children and caring for them to within a few hours of her death, also died. Meanwhile their grandmother Stuart had died. Phelps was now twelve years old. At this time, of her own will, she joined the church, perhaps seeking support comparable to that which her mother had found in angelic recorders. (One newspaper eulogist dates this, rather than her mother's death, as the time when she changed her name.[29]) Undoubtedly such a succession of deaths— of her grandfather, mother, grandmother, and aunt-stepmother— made life seem a precarious venture for an eight- to twelve-year-old child. Both of her parents had recorded childhood preoccupation with death; neither was a robustly healthy person. Young Phelps herself stated that she had "less than usual physical vigor" (*Chapters*, 61). Her childhood experience of death and illness both would become material for novels written in adulthood.

Perhaps the 1858 marriage of Austin Phelps to Mary Ann Johnson (1830–1918), sister of an Andover clergyman, stabilized thirteen-year-old Phelps's environment. Reportedly the new mother first saw her stepdaughter with eyes "intent upon a group of girls eagerly listening to a story from her lips."[30] Apparently this young mother from Boston exhibited the full array of social skills expected of an ideal hostess-wife. Phelps noted that she owed many "gentle lessons" to this "kind and conscientious new mother," but although the "new mother" had "no small part in forming her character," her real mother, "obliged to go to heaven when she seemed so necessary in Andover," nonetheless influenced her daughter's lifework (*Chapters*, 11, 104).

Aspirations of Authorship

Phelps recalled that she was not precocious, unlike her father, but rather a tomboy—like another popular writer in her childhood, Louisa May Alcott. She enjoyed climbing to the top of an apple tree or walking the length of the seminary fence more than serious writing or reading. She considered herself an outdoor girl, who appreciated her father's gardens. Not a scholar, she nonetheless preferred to stand near the top of her class, from pride rather than from intellect. Mrs. Edwards' School for Young Ladies offered a college curriculum in all but Greek and trigonometry, then considered beyond feminine intellect. Phelps wondered at the breadth of this curriculum, since the school's Andover faculty advisers (her father among them) held rather "feudal views" of women. She concluded, however, that Mrs. Edwards, as the school's strong and learned principal, must have had ideas of her own, which accounted for its rigor. Phelps knew one other Andover female type, the unmarried woman. Such were viewed, however, as "feminine triumphs." Clearly not lacking for suitors in a town the proportion of whose "masculine society was almost Western in its munificence," they had "of free will absolute...passed through life alone (*Chapters*, 29). In

Andover singleness in the eyes of its girls carried with it an aura of victory!

For all the achievement of its female residents, Andover was doubtful of their capacity. Austin Phelps—believing that there was "only so much of a *girl*" (he accepted then-current views of limited female energy) and knowing his daughter was of doubtful health—directed her to "give the best of herself to her studies" (*Chapters*, 61). Out of context, this seems no doubt good advice, but given with the cutting edge of derogation (from his belief in a naturally limited female intellect), it became a message exhorting achievement while questioning its possibility. Nonetheless, Phelps traced her intellectual awakening at sixteen to her father's reading of essays by De Quincey and poems by Wordsworth. His conversation, and the education that he therein transmitted, Phelps found to have been as interesting to her as anything in later life: "he talked a great deal," she wrote, "not to us, but with us." He was a "consecrated man": it was not possible to have such a father and not believe in a heavenly Father (*Chapters*, 53, 58-59). Phelps followed her mother in her adulation of a patriarchal father, an earthly representative of Final Authority. Both women wished their writing to be approved by their fathers before anyone else. They unduly elevated both men—a fact that could only have made each woman feel inadequate. On the other hand, since fathers were expected to act as household authorities—in these instances, as both religious and pedagogical authorities—they could not have hesitated, without discrediting themselves, from assuming a stance of mastery. The more masterful appeared the man, the more dependent upon him must the woman feel. Thus fathers and daughters were caught in patterns of self-defeating behavior, unfortunately reinforced by culture-wide expectations.

The awakening of her own literary aspirations and her recognition of her own nature Phelps ascribed to her reading, when she was still sixteen, of Elizabeth Barrett Browning's blank verse novel *Aurora Leigh* (1856) (*Chapters*, 64-66). It is perhaps instructive to consider briefly the content of a work that had so great an impact upon young Phelps. Not only does Phelps discuss its impact in her autobiography, but she makes it pivotal also in the life of her favorite woman character, the heroine in her novel *The Story of Avis* (1877). Barrett Browning, in *Aurora Leigh*, presents a portrait of the artist as a young woman, as would Phelps some two decades later. The problems confronting the young woman Aurora on the brink of her poetic career are deeply personal: because she is female, her very capacity to write poetry is questioned by her cousin and suitor, Romney Leigh (Book II);[31] she should, he tells her, devote herself to a man as his wife and to his work as helpmate. This discussion, satirizing typical arguments denigrating woman's capacity, concludes with Aurora's puzzled dismay at his asking to lean upon her who is believed unable to stand alone! (Book II) Aurora rejects this man's proposal in order to pursue, very successfully, her own career in London (Books III, V). After a fire that leaves him blind, Romney once again proposes marriage (Book VIII). This time Aurora accepts: a chastened man aware of the limitations of his own authority might join with a woman, each to take up their chosen work for the world (Book IX).

Interestingly, Barrett Browning divides the roles of mother and wife between two characters. The conflict within one woman between the roles of artist and wife Barrett Browning resolves by granting the artist the time needed to develop her identity independent of a husband's expectations. Phelps in *The Story of Avis* would show how becoming a wife before establishing an artistic career could be disastrous for the career. Barrett Browning's clear and confident portrayal of a woman with a vocation spoke to the experience of sixteen-year-old Phelps, who had watched her own mother stagger under the burdens of child-rearing, household management, and a literary career. She would in her later fiction address herself to the troubles of her time. If her sex forbade her entering the pulpit to follow in the footsteps of her forefathers, she would—after the models of her foremothers—use her pen to produce novels, if not sermons, for the reformation of her world.

Chapter Two
A Heavenly Utopia—
Haven for Women

The 1860s constituted a period of emerging self-consciousness in the life of Elizabeth Stuart Phelps. At sixteen she had been aroused by the story of Aurora Leigh's fulfillment first as a writer and then as a wife, a pattern Phelps would imitate. Phelps's early work suggests her belief that a girl, to fully realize herself, needed the support of a strong woman. To depict this necessity Phelps developed three types of characters: a benefactress, a needful woman, and a self-supporting woman. The types could merge into each other. A benefactress must be self-supporting in order to be effective, and if she were effective, a needful woman became a self-supporting woman. The three types seem to represent needs that Phelps herself experienced during the decade. Where her early characterizations in Sunday school stories reflect public expectations, later more complex characters begin to reveal her inner needs and suggest the theme of self-fulfillment for women.

This theme, a crucial ingredient in her most popular fiction, was common as well to antebellum nineteenth-century Utopian communities. In fact, the emancipation of women was of prime concern to all (except German) communal groups in existence in the United States from 1680 to 1880. In general, such groups were concerned that women have rights equal to men's, that domestic chores be kept to a minimum, that husbands avoid drunkenness and improvidence, and that a stimulating communal life exist for both sexes.[1]

This American Utopianism, expressed frequently in communal experimentation before the Civil War, appeared more often in idealistic literature afterward. Utopian writers between 1888 (the date of Edward Bellamy's *Looking Backward, 2000–1887*) and 1900 show both discontent with the status quo and longing for society based upon an ideal family structure—one incorporating, however, traditional gender roles. This ideal family structure took three forms: (1) the conventional, nuclear Victorian family; (2) a structure that, while freeing women from economic dependence upon men, anticipated women's continued child-rearing and sexual services to men; and (3) an ideal family that eliminated both economic and social functions to ensure the convention of chastity.[2] Phelps shared the discontent, but rather than solving problems of family structure by imagining conditions designed to create ideal wives and mothers, she reformed husbands and fathers by requiring their participation in housekeeping and child-rearing.

Where antebellum Utopian practice took the form of positive social experimentation, postbellum practice concentrated on discontent with a deteriorating social milieu. During the late nineteenth century the combination of industrialization and urbanization became the greatest single determining factor in American life, a factor that had dislocated, and thus disoriented, large segments of the population. Thus the period from 1890s to the 1920s was a transition between cultural systems. When anarchy seems most a threat, the Utopian genre flourishes. Research into women's lives at this time shows ever-increasing fragmentation: the disruption of family relations and friendships increased, and the distance between the men who controlled institutions and the women who allegedly benefited grew. Some two decades before the bulk of this Utopian writing Phelps anticipated the need to question the changes then in process. Her Utopian vision stressed not social structure or technological power, but emotional structure—the extent to which self-fulfillment was encouraged. Phelps retained in her Utopian fiction the concern of earlier Utopian communities: her heavenly Utopia would provide a haven in which women might realize their potential.

In addition to societal factors leading to Utopian speculation, Phelps experienced pressures in her own life that also may have motivated her to consider how women might enjoy lives more satisfactory than those she had seen.

Personal Pressures

A particular happiness Phelps's life might have included, but which the Civil War took from her, was a relationship with a young man. She had become a close friend of Samuel Hopkins Thompson, Class of 1861 at Phillips Academy.[3] He enlisted in the spring of 1861. By October 22, 1862, he lay dead in a hospital of wounds incurred at the battle of Antietam. "What tenderest of men [Austin Phelps?] knows how to comfort his own daughter [herself?] when her heart is broken?" Phelps later asked (*Chapters*, 98). If being a wife was the status expected of women, if it was to promote womanly happiness, then losing a potential husband would clearly have seemed disaster, the possibility for such happiness perhaps permanently lost.[4]

Either after Thompson's death or after completing school, Phelps suffered ill health. Her own writing illuminates the relationship between leaving school and becoming an invalid. Responding to the infamous Dr. E. H. Clarke's *Sex in Education* (1873), Phelps notes that, contrary to Clarke's position, girls are healthy while occupied with school and become sick only after leaving.[5] She offers numerous explanations: plunging from "brain exertion" to "completed education," exchanging the pursuit of goals for unrelieved domestic routine, changing from expecting "life would be something" to realizing it would be nothing, being inspired to develop herself then finding she cannot continue, being deprived of vocational stimulus except in marriage "which she may never effect, and which may never help the matter if she does," and "being happy" then "being miserable" (*Sex*, 135-36). Drawing upon her own and her mother's experience as well as upon her observations of Andover school girls, Phelps proclaims, "The sense of perplexed disappointment, of baffled intelligence, of unoccupied powers, of blunted aspirations ... is enough to create any illness which nervous wear and misery can create" (*Sex*, 137).

In addition to health, several domestic circumstances hindered Phelps's development as a writer. In 1860 her stepbrother, Francis Johnson Phelps, was born. Her youngest brother—Edward

Johnson Phelps, the "Trotty" of two juvenile books—arrived in 1863. So many small boys required seemingly endless sewing chores of her who never enjoyed domestic duties. In addition, the boys were noisy, "a definite check to inspiration" (*Chapters*, 101-2). Even harder to bear, she had no hospitable place to write. She tells of carrying on "the writer's profession for many years as if it had been a burglar's," of seeking quiet in attic, closet, or haymow, and warmth under her mother's old fur cape (*Chapters*, 82, 103). During the 1860s no one took seriously a girl's apprenticeship. Against such a backdrop Phelps accomplished her early writing.

During her years at Mrs. Edwards' School for Young Ladies, Phelps and an unnamed "dearest particular intimate" had shared with each other chapters from their manuscript novels—Phelps writing no less than three, one melodramatically entitled "The Shadow of a Lifetime" (*Chapters*, 74-75). But these were lost and their content forgotten. The work Phelps labeled as her beginning was a war story, "A Sacrifice Consumed," likely deriving from the loss of Thompson. Appearing in *Harper's New Monthly Magazine* in January, 1864, it concerns a seamstress who, having lost her fiancé at Antietam, wonders how his war contribution could be "worth all this suffering."[6] Austin Phelps's pleasure at this accomplishment was, she wrote, "only equaled by [his] frank and unqualified astonishment. ... [Like her mother, she felt] ten hundred thousand unknown voices could not move me to the pride and pleasure which my father's first gentle word of approval gave to a girl who cared much to be loved and little to be praised" (*Chapters*, 76). Lacking self-confidence, she notes that had her early stories been refused she would not have written more. Contrary to convention, she acknowledged the pleasure of economic independence that such stories gave her: believing it "too easy to be dependent upon too heavily-weighted and too generous men," she stated, "I am proud to say that I have always been a working woman, and always had to be" (*Chapters*, 79).

Phelps's desire for independence in a society that encouraged the reverse for its women was shared as well by others. From the first National Women Rights Convention held in Worcester,

Massachusetts, October 23 and 24, 1850, a movement in her state for the emancipation of women gathered momentum. At the end of the 1860s Phelps published her first articles concerning women's status, and during the 1870s became a contributor to the Massachusetts-based weekly newspaper, the *Woman's Journal*.

Her Apprenticeship, 1860–1867

From 1860 to 1867 Phelps learned to support herself by writing, a profession she considered poor in monetary return. As she could not "live by bread or magazine articles alone," she did Sunday school "hack work" (*Chapters*, 81). Signing herself "E. Stuart Phelps," like her mother after establishing her literary credit, the younger Phelps wrote in 1864 two of a four-volume "Tiny" series, concerning the efforts of five-year-old Tiny to "be good" and eleven-year-old Ellen to "become Christian."[7] Typical of contemporary Sunday school stories, "God" here seems to have been shorthand for obedience to socially sanctioned authority.

Whereas the "Tiny" set urges its readers to become "Christian," a second set ("Gypsy") would urge them to become "ladylike."[8] Phelps considered both sets Sunday school books; save for the age difference of their audiences, their aims were similar. Thus "ladylike" simply replaces "Christian" as the term for proper feminine behavior. The vocabulary is secularized, but the behavior patterns remain unchanged.

In using ordinary daily life as the material with which to illustrate such desired behavior, Phelps in this second set of four books followed her mother's *Little Mary* (1854). In the first story the twelve-year-old heroine, Gypsy Breynton, tries to remember to "do right" in spite of her tomboy inclinations. In the second she shares the pleasures of country living with her city cousin. In the third she helps her college-aged brother "keep straight." In the fourth she attempts to become a "perfect lady" at boarding school in spite of her girl friend's bad example. Typical of incidents in the "Gypsy" books is one in which Gypsy, having climbed into a tree to complete her mending, jumps down without noticing that in landing she will upset her father's garden statue. Gypsy's mother believes her careless, but her father thinks her jumping from a tree—an act she could easily perform—unfitting for a girl (*G. Breynton*, 124). The series ends with Gypsy's conviction that she is a "hopeless case" and will "never learn to be proper" (*Crescent*, 261). She is one of Phelps's earliest victims of society's expectations: Gypsy believes she is a failure, when in fact she has been asked to become the impossible.

During 1865 Phelps published two books for older girls, *Mercy Gliddon's Work* and *Up Hill; or Life in the Factory*, and also wrote, "Jane Gurley's Story," serialized from March to October, 1866, in *Hours at Home*. All three stories reflect Phelps's intellectual and social concerns, likewise articulated in *The Gates Ajar*, and foreshadow her later writing.

In *Mercy Gliddon's Work*, of the three the book least related to *The Gates Ajar*, Phelps directly confronts the problem of defining women's work.[9] For Phelps at this time, wishing to progress as a writer yet restrained by responsibilities to her father's household, such definition was urgent. Although Mercy's case and her creator's differ in detail, the options are the same—heroic work versus home duty. Phelps's book opens with Mercy hearing of a war nurse just returned from the battlefront. Deciding that this suits her, too, Mercy volunteers, though her friend ridicules her view of herself as a "saint" off to nurse sick soldiers (*Mercy*, 83). Such unromantic duties as unpacking bandages in a cold entryway also puncture Mercy's notion of heroic and glorious war work. Finally, she becomes ill from the doctors' insensitively overworking her. When Mercy learns that her mother has contracted brain fever from the nightly care of sick children, she determines that it is her "duty to recover" and return home—reminiscent of the death of Phelps's mother, who had referred to her "duty to live" that she might continue the care of her children (*Mercy*, 193, 196).[10]

But Phelps qualifies this advocacy of home duty. In a discussion with her mother, Mercy asks whether women must only stay home, sew, wash dishes, and teach Sunday school, and whether women who never marry and "have gifts for positive work in the world" must "stifle with unsatisfied tasks" (*Mercy*, 227). Mrs.

Gliddon responds, "If a woman's tastes lead her from home and she can be spared, she should be spared, and should go." She continues that more could be spared than are, but that the question is too intricate to be answered by a rule; a woman must judge for herself and no one has any right to deny her (*Mercy*, 227-28). Through comments of both a neighbor and the minister's wife, Phelps provides public support in the story for Mercy's being excused from domestic duties. Set against this principle, the illness of Mercy and her mother may address Phelps's own psychic needs and her estimate of her audience's expectations: a conservative, self-sacrificing solution appropriate to an Andover professor's daughter and the typical role for women respected by her audience.

Mercy's home duty, however, can expand beyond her immediate relatives to include a larger human community. In the Gliddons's maid Judy—the first of a succession of Irish servants sympathetically presented in Phelps's work—Mercy finds a person she can help. Discovering that Judy's mother is dying, Mercy sends her home. Later Mercy teaches Judy to read. Thus, at the end of this first book, Phelps begins to develop what for her are to be frequent character-types—benefactress and needful woman. Such charity, as an extension of home duty, is, she implies, more useful than participation in a "heroic" war. The first and also the youngest example of this character, Mercy is followed by successively older women, as Phelps develops the stages of such a career.

Both *Up Hill* and "Jane Gurley's Story" continue the exploration of the woman who, through either work or philanthropy, "does good" in the world. In earlier versions such a character accomplishes what a man could not: she is a superior savior of others. For example, in *Up Hill; or Life in the Factory*, not the Sunday school principal but the teacher Miss Grant guides the Christian progress of mill girls Mary Kirk and Kate Bradley.[11] Phelps thus feminizes an originally male-centered religious pattern and demonstrates to readers that the total range of human possibilities might now be shared by members of both sexes, rather than presumed by the male sex. In fact, the guardianship of morality then attributed to women exemplifies a way in which

American religion had been placed under feminine control. If the work of middle-class women ceased to have economic value, their presence at home nonetheless provided moral guardianship. But in households where, in the absence of a male breadwinner, the female breadwinners must work away from home and could not provide full-time guardianship, a "superfluous" single woman might then create for herself a new public role of providing such guardianship. Miss Grant, the Sunday school teacher of *Up Hill*, and her successors among Phelps's women characters demonstrate such moral guardianship in a more public sphere than their own private households and make private spheres the settings for public guidance.

Probably based upon Phelps's own experience teaching Sunday school in Abbot Village, Miss Grant provides moral support to the two mill girls. Their families are very different. Mary Kirk is fortunate in having a mother's moral guidance, even though she and her younger sister support the fatherless household by millwork; with three small children the widowed Mrs. Kirk has little time to fill the needlework orders that are her only means of breadwinning. Kate Bradley, on the other hand, though both parents are alive, receives little guidance: her father is a drunken "wreck of what had once been a man" (56) and her refined mother is untrained to deal effectively with impoverishment. Though the God to whom Kate and Mary must "break their wills" (220) is one of love, their religious training, albeit administered by a woman, constitutes adaptation to a subordinate social position and unquestioning acceptance of God's authoritative concern for them. For example, Miss Grant tells Kate that all she need do is keep God's "commandments" (153). The Christian conduct expected of both girls is the willing acceptance of their secondary and supportive roles—Mary of her mother and Kate of her brother. Phelps places the burden for improving lives more upon personal piety than upon expanding a confining environment (the view she would later hold).

Although Phelps does not stress this environment, she does show that little opportunity for development exists. She emphasizes how young girls are brutalized by inadequate mental stimulation and by confinement in ill-ventilated and noisy workrooms.

In addition, a distant Civil War, which the lower-class women and men are powerless to control, takes away the meagre chance the women have for a better life by killing, imprisoning, or maiming their breadwinners: women earn lower and less reliable wages than men and can not obtain training for more lucrative employment. Even Miss Grant, for all her encouragement of her protegées' piety, seems finally a rich lady dispensing, and thereby justifying, her own largesse, rather than a woman seeking to strengthen the fabric of others' lives as in Phelps's later work. Miss Grant teaches the submissiveness that will make mill girls more manipulable workers: like religious training in the "Tiny" series, such behavior discourages self-realization. Miss Grant does, however, treat mill girls as human beings worthy of her respectful concern, contrary to many mill owners who saw them as mere "hands." By extending to them the hospitality of her own parlor, she eliminates the boundary between domestic and public sphere and thereby completes the interpenetration of the two.

Phelps's tendency to treat women of low social status realistically and nonjudgmentally and those of higher status idealistically and approvingly is less marked here than in "Jane Gurley's Story."[12] In the latter, Miss Grant's older counterpart, Miss Granger, becomes Jane Gurley's savior. The Gurley family has problems far more serious even than those of the Bradley family in *Up Hill*. The more severe the problems, however, the more potency can be ascribed to the person able to surmount them.

In the early chapters Phelps establishes the confining nature of Jane's environment and the difficulty of escaping its claims. With her alcoholic-gambler father, opium-addict mother, and baby brother Ben, Jane lives in the sordid neighborhood of an urban waterfront. She is an "artist sealed in silence," a loom-worker whose "clamorous wants" are stifled (2:499). Above all, she desires the training that will release her pent-up creative needs (2:500). Phelps combines in Jane the problems of Mercy Gliddon and the *Up Hill* mill girls: she must both find her proper work and cope with mill-town deprivations. At first Jane believes she has found a solution in the love between her and Reuben Trull: they share a dream of escape with Ben to a country home. But foul play and a train accident take Reuben's life. Jane's problem then becomes how to overcome despair. Without Reuben's companionship and with responsibility for Ben, she heads aimlessly for the country, in search of Reuben's God. A feminized God and savior appears in the person of Miss Granger, a benefactress who recognizes Jane's stifled longings and undeveloped artistic skill.

Not her minister-father, but Miss Granger herself, a feminized God-deputy, effects Jane's fulfillment. Rather than hiring Jane as a servant, thereby keeping her dependent upon charity, Miss Granger enables her to make a living from commercial art. By designing wallpaper for a local manufactory, Jane becomes self-supporting and continues her care of Ben. Phelps allows Jane Gurley to escape, unlike Mercy Gliddon, who must accommodate to middle-class domestic duties, or the *Up Hill* mill girls, who learn submission to lower-class deprivation. In Jane, Phelps adds a third to her two character types of benefactress and benefited— namely, the woman who finds an unconventional, yet for her entirely suitable, means of supporting herself. Jane, like the maid Judy and the *Up Hill* mill girls, exemplifies a woman who needs help and thus justifies the existence of a benefactress.

During the mid-1860s the character-types—benefited, benefactress, and self-supporter—seem to express needs that Phelps would have experienced. We might reasonably speculate how each type would have provided Phelps such expression. First, as compensation for maternal loss, she imagined a strong woman encouraging young women's independence. Next, to gain approval from a father she worshipped, she imagined women ministering publicly to the needs of others but, at the same time, by way of rebelling against his "feudal views," she imagined women demonstrating their superior potency in this role. By the 1870s, to reinforce her own assertion of financial independence, she began to imagine women following increasingly successful paths comparable to her own.

Her Popular Works, 1868–1887

While the Sunday school books were still in progress, Phelps began at the end of 1864 the book that would establish her literary career: *The Gates Ajar* (1868). The advice of Annie

Adams Fields (1834-1915)—wife of the publisher James T. Fields (1817-1881), and future friend of Phelps—resulted in its publication after a two-year delay. Soon afterwards James T. Fields wrote Phelps that, "Your book is moving grandly. It has already reached a sale of four thousand copies" (*Chapters*, 109). By 1897 *The Gates Ajar* had reached 81,000 copies in print in the United States; by 1900, in England, slightly over 100,000 copies. Translations appeared in German, French, Dutch, and Italian.

The Gates Ajar was the first of a series of three books, each suggesting that a Utopian heaven would compensate for earthly suffering after we pass through "the gates" separating this life from an afterlife. These "Gates" books were her most popular— the works by which she was internationally known and for which mail-order catalogs anticipated a ready sale. As a group they provide both an overview of Phelps's work and a demonstration of her covert criticism of woman's place, couched as heavenly Utopia.

In each of the three stories published during the writing of *The Gates Ajar* Phelps had given progressively greater consideration to the dilemma of having to live in a world where loved ones die. A subplot in *Mercy Gliddon's Work* concerns the death of a young soldier who never declared his love, a circumstance apparently identical with that of Phelps's friend Thompson. In *Up Hill* a brother is reported killed in action. The emotional pattern— anticipated happiness, dashed hope, and resultant despair—of "Jane Gurley's Story," although disguised in a lower-class setting, repeats Phelps's experience in Thompson's death. In each instance the bereaved regains hope through belief in a Savior who will provide a heavenly reunion. These peripheral treatments of death are closer to Phelps's experience than that of *The Gates Ajar*: though living with the grief caused by death is the sole concern of the book, the death is that of an older brother, an instance far from her own life. But imagining a brother's death rather than a lover's may have given Phelps the psychic distance necessary to harness her pain to constructive use, since a brother would typically have less impact upon a woman's future than a husband. Moreover, casting her response to Thompson's death as if that of a sister for a brother would have deflected public speculation from her private life. In addition, she had the model of another author's recasting the death of her husband as that of a brother: British novelist Margaret Oliphant (1828–1897) had used this device in *A Son of the Soil* (1866), to which Phelps refers in *The Gates Ajar*.[13]

In addition to her personal experience, the national impact of Civil War carnage sparked Phelps's concern. She wrote regarding her purpose in *The Gates Ajar* that she wanted to comfort "the bereaved wife, mother, sister, and widowed girl"; that she thought of "the women...they whom the war trampled down, without a choice or protest; the patient, limited, domestic women, who thought little but loved much, and, loving, had lost all" (*Chapters*, 97-98). She felt "prevailing beliefs" had little to say that could help an "afflicted woman," since "creeds and commentaries and sermons were made by men" (*Chapters*, 98). Although she disclaimed sympathy at the time with any public "movement for the peculiar needs of women as a class," her own experience and her recognition of other women's needs lay behind the book (*Chapters*, 99). Perhaps this universal sensitivity accounts for the popularity of the "Gates" books in lands where no Civil War had occurred.

Phelps claimed yet another inspiration for the book: "The angel said unto me 'Write!' and I wrote" (*Chapters*, 99). But such inspiration she herself contradicted by observing that she spent two or three solitary years reading "what had been written for the mourning" as well as expending "steady and conscientious toil" (*Chapters*, 100). That she should have emulated Harriet Beecher Stowe's explanation for the inspiration of *Uncle Tom's Cabin* (1852) is not surprising. An Andover neighbor from 1851 until 1864, Stowe was a model of female success and a woman writer who made her novels into sermons advocating the reformation of social ills and urging the recognition of human needs. In *The Minister's Wooing* (1859) she also had written a critique of an uncomprehending clergy. Like *The Gates Ajar*, the book assuages a personal grief—the 1857 drowning of her son Henry—though, like Phelps, Stowe presented in her narrative not that personal event but the 1822 drowning of her sister's fiancé. Even closer to Phelps than the example of Stowe was her own mother's writing *The Sunny Side; or, the Country Minister's Wife* (1852) to memorialize a departed friend. Unlike the novels of Stowe and the younger Phelps, *The Sunny Side* does not expressly concern death, but rather presents a "sunny" account of the memorialized life. Even given these literary models that suggest the appropriateness of labeling *The Gates Ajar* as consolation literature, the label, though not inaccurate, is inadequate.[14]

This inadequacy becomes apparent when we examine the book's implicit social criticism. A minister's widow, Winifred Forceythe, is the potent and successful attendant to the needs of bereaved woman and man. That Phelps unreservedly gave to a woman capacity usually invested in men stands in clear contrast to the inferior status accorded women she knew. This theme of women's success, couched in conventional beliefs in the existence of a Benevolent Male Diety and Heavenly Afterlife, must have appealed to politically powerless women because, though not contradicting religious convention, it implied serious criticism of women's earthly status. Unfortunately, however, the book's hopeful emphasis upon otherworldly rewards may have had the dubious result of easing accommodation to an unrewarding present. Phelps could not yet resolve this ambivalence regarding women's success.

The Gates Ajar takes the form of a journal in which one Mary Cabot records her mourning and her growth toward emotional independence. With the death of her brother Roy in the Civil War, Mary initially feels desolate at being a solitary orphan. Not until the arrival of her widowed Aunt Winifred Forceythe with her three-and-a-half-year-old daughter Faith does Mary begin to overcome her despair. Through successive dialogues with Winifred, each carefully recorded in her journal, Mary learns to live with her loss. Rather than the clergy's cold doctrine, Winifred offers a consoling theology adjusted to the needs of troubled human beings who need relief from anguish. Sometimes her theology is behavioral rather than verbal: for example, cradling Mary in her lap as if she were a child. At other times she urges

Mary to ignore the views of Deacon Quirk and the minister Dr. Bland that she pay lip service to the forms of properly pious behavior. Winifred thus assumes her own capacity to interpret the ways of God to woman.

Like Mercy Gliddon, Winifred finds "God's great and glorious work" in the immediate needs of those about her. For Mary's consolation, she particularizes a view of an earthly world where Roy's spirit still exists to comfort her and a heavenly home where Mary will eventually join him. Foreshadowing the Utopian vision that Phelps would develop in *Beyond the Gates* (1883), Winifred speaks of "new tastes and capacities" which would be "enlarged" in one's heavenly existence (76). Belief in a heavenly afterlife, interpreted as compensation for earthly loss or lack, was calculated to relieve bereavement. Contemporary clergy accusing Phelps of "heresy...and atrocity" missed her point, namely, to create a system that could console women for their loss, not only of loved ones, but of fulfillment as well.[15]

In addition to transmitting a view of heaven as compensation for earthly ills, Winifred like her predecessor Miss Granger gives others life in her ability to know how best to develop each individual's self-confidence. By acknowledging and responding with support to others' needs she enhances their self-esteem. Mary's journal records her growth from a state of despondence over losing the man upon whom she had relied to one of autonomy without him. Even more striking is Winifred's impact upon Dr. Bland, whose doctrine is proven inadequate in the face of his wife's death. After Winifred's sympathetic ministry to him, he gives "pleasant, helpful" sermons wholly unlike his previously irrelevant performances (147). Winifred's "womanliness" resides in her capacity to bring about changes through loving acceptance, a demonstration of Phelps's belief that "Infinite Power and Mercy are one" (*Chapters*, 130).

In Winifred, Phelps embodies an ideal of Christian womanhood. Like *Up Hill, The Gates Ajar* is a story of Christian progress, here shown in the change that Winifred has the power to effect in Mary. By the time Winifred dies, Mary has become inwardly strong enough to maintain adequately her own life as well as that of Winifred's daughter Faith. Like Miss Granger for Jane Gurley, Mary Cabot will provide a sure foundation for Faith's emotional growth. What Phelps advocates is behavior that supports the development of others, rather than that which exacts its own support from others. Perhaps her opportunity as a child to observe men requiring their wives' emotional support partly explains her capacity as an adult to perceive what those wives had lacked in self-fulfillment.

Subsequent "Gates" books elaborate the heavenly Utopia suggested by Winifred in *The Gates Ajar*—a Utopia where self-fulfillment occurs. Although Phelps was adamant that the "Gates" books not be advertised as sequels, we can best examine them as a series because the books of 1883 and 1887 successively amplify her theme.[16]

Although Phelps developed her plan for *Beyond the Gates* immediately after the publication of *The Gates Ajar*, fifteen years elapsed before she actually wrote it.[17] In the first "Gates" book Phelps assures her audience of reunion with loved relatives and depicts successful female ministry. In *Beyond the Gates* (1883) she offers women the expectation of heavenly self-fulfillment and reliable male support. Using the convention of a dream vision, she places a dying woman into the arms of her deceased father. Mary, forty years old, unconscious with brain fever, envisions a heavenly existence: her dead father has been housekeeping alone, awaiting the arrival of his earthly family, a reversal requiring a man to learn in heaven the life-maintaining activities left to women on earth. Mary recounts that, though unmarried, she had not been unhappy in her life, but rather had been vigorously active in teaching, traveling, nursing, and social work—an inventory of acceptable public activities for women. All of these occupations concerned "more largely the experience of other people than ... [her] own" (7). What she had missed, her vision of heaven reveals.

Phelps does not emphasize the economic or technological wonders of a heavenly Utopia, but rather imagines a society that supports the self-fulfillment of its members. Since Mary had been helping others to fulfillment, she must now learn to know her own "whole nature" and follow its dictates (41). All of her senses—sight, touch, hearing—are enhanced in the new environment: she finds she has sensuous capacities—for example, to see color and hear music—she had not realized before. Winifred of *The Gates Ajar* had predicted such "enlarged capacities" (76).

Looking in upon her earthbound family, Mary sees they appear unhappy and possessed by great unrest. She finds that, contrary to earthly existence, in heaven a woman can rest. Also, pleasure exists in more intense and diverse modes than on earth: Mary dares to be happy and finds this daring the very spirit of her daily living. She learns to risk, but gains happiness from the resulting growth.

In agreement with Phelps's earlier novels showing that God's "glorious work" lies close to home, the heavenly celebrity is she who unknown has given lifelong devotion to an unpopular philosophy or she whose family has leaned upon her strength "like infants" innocent of the demands they make (147). In addition, people speak to "carry comfort to the hearts of some," no matter if an "imperfect manner of expression...offend the heads of others" (133). Further, Phelps wishes to reform men of their unrecognized earthly oversights; for example, she shows little admiration for fame not tempered by kindness or for elegant words not imbued with compassion.

Besides pleading for self-fulfillment and for rewarding the unrecognized, *Beyond the Gates* offers strong social criticism. From her knowledge of mill-town existence, Phelps includes, as compensation for rampant deprivation, automatic access in heaven to whatever residences, recreation, education, or hospitalization citizens of a Utopian city might require to correct the earthly deficits with which they arrive. Phelps objects to the effect of urban industrialization upon human lives.

The book closes, however, upon a more individual note. Toward the end of her vision, Mary, after being joined by her mother, finds filial love inadequate for a mature person. Meeting again a man whom she might have loved twenty years ago, she rejoices in his "claiming" her. But awakening from her dream, Mary says "'Oh, Mother, I have Heaven in my heart at last'"—

then realizes that Heaven is no more (194). That Phelps returns
Mary to health and disappointment suggests the emptiness of
Mary's earlier claim that she was happy though unmarried. (In a
letter written May 14, 1882, Phelps noted that she ought to have
married when young in order to avoid later loneliness.)[18]

But we need reconsider Mary's disappointment in the continu-
ation of her former not-unhappy life. Did her various occupations seem unsatisfactory to her only since a heavenly vision had
shown her what had been lacking, that her busyness was a foil for
loneliness? Or was it that conventional expectations for a
woman—that she marry and bear children—by their mere definition of the activities proper for women, made her miss the
pleasure of her own life's accomplishments? Possibly public taste
dictated Phelps's conclusion to this book—that she find an
unmarried woman unhappy. But her fiction would never show a
married woman happy.

Beyond the Gates is devastating social criticism. Precisely what
is wished provides an index of what women missed and suggests
why they flocked to read the "Gates" books. Phelps represents
Heaven as offering to women what earth lacked—namely, men
prepared as adults to nurture the lives of women and children,
and opportunities for women to experience pleasure, self-
fulfillment, and the companionship of equals. For women particularly, "to be dead was to be alive to a sense of assured good
chance that nothing in the universe could shake" (72). Two other
women would have concurred. Margaret Fuller (1810–1850)
wrote that she saw "no way out except through the gate of
death."[19] And the novelist Kate Chopin (1851–1904) in Edna
Pontellier of *The Awakening* (1899) depicted death preserving a
woman from a dehumanizing and fragmented existence. If we
label these first two "Gates" books consolation literature, then we
must understand the consolatory effect to include compensation
not only for the death of loved ones, but also for deprivation in all
the forms that women experienced.

In the third book of the series, *The Gates Between* (1887),
Phelps made the central character not female but male, the

physician Esmerald Thorne.[20] Her characterization of Esmerald reveals both her ideal and her critique. Having considered reunion with loved ones in the first book and provision of denied fulfillment and companionship in the second, Phelps turned her attention to the heavenly reform of an inconsiderate husband—a theme leading the *Woman's Journal* to offer the book as a subscription premium.[21] Given the earthly patriarchal structure of nineteenth-century families, Phelps located in heaven fulfillment for women and reform of their male partners.

Using the device of a communication from the Other Side, Phelps in Esmerald's narration reveals that reform.[22] Esmerald is catapulted into heaven from an accident caused by his runaway horse. His enjoyment of his own power had led him to own a disastrously fast horse and had also blinded him to his other deficiencies. As Mary in heaven discovers her life unfulfilled, so Esmerald finds his underdeveloped. First he realizes that he has had an unwholesome habit of classifying women as "neuralgic, hysteric, dyspeptic" rather than as "unselfish, intelligent, high-minded" (5). Then he perceives that as a boy he was spoiled in having been trained to believe that only the male has the liberty to speak freely what he thinks; by middle age he had trusted his power and charm to compensate for irritability or uncontrolled anger. Hence, Esmerald's healthy wife Helen had found that her former strength dissolved as she learned to wait both for and upon her husband. Phelps connects the love of power explicit in Esmerald's behavior to ignorance of conditions encouraging the development of human potential.

Having discovered his shortcomings, Esmerald sets upon a course of re-socialization and domestication. No longer able to control others, he must learn to wait for their compliance. He finds his own humanity narrowly trained to the intellectual: a patient's capacity to love proves more lasting than his to control. To learn the ways of loving nurture, Esmerald receives the care of his now-deceased son, about whose former illness he had found his wife overly concerned. He who loved fame, power, and love itself must perform sundry invisible acts in support of his son's life—"lowly tasks [men] left...to women in the world below" (185). Esmerald acknowledges his inadequacy as a parent: others have sight where he is blind.

Once recognizing his deficiencies as husband, physician, and father, Esmerald can increase his vision. Where he had previously longed only to see Helen, he now desires to cultivate kindness in all earthly homes. He longs to increase human sensitivity to the power of words—of loving words to support, of cruel words to harm. Thus, he becomes worthy of his wife's heavenly companionship. At last Helen "clung to [him] because she could not help it, and would not if she could"(222).

Helen, merely a foil to Esmerald, is subordinated even in heaven as she "crept" to him. Phelps, concentrating upon a male character, seems less able to question such subordination than when she had placed a female character at the center of a plot. Apparently the presence of masculinity so overwhelmed her that femininity automatically fell into its shadow even when her aim as here was to equalize the relationship between the sexes. Characterization in both *Beyond the Gates* and *The Gates Between* shows that each sex could and must learn the strengths of the other because only thus might we fully experience our humanity. Where two gender roles had existed, Phelps implies one—that of realizing full human potential, regardless of sex.

In 1901 Phelps published her last "Gates" book, a dramatization of her 1887 novel, now called *Within the Gates*. Originally serialized in *McClure's Magazine*, it was never staged.[23] In it Phelps draws more sharply the lines contrasting the behavior of husband and wife so as to emphasize the husband's error in being unsupportive. Also, in several minor characters she openly criticizes the medical profession—for vivisection practices and for professional ethics that benefit doctors but not patients. For example, to Dr. Carver's ordering unnecessary surgery and Dr. Gazell's lighthearted decision that a woman's irritability requires operative cure, Phelps contrasts Dr. Thorne's diagnosis for the patient's benefit and a nurse's sharp observation that Gazell's policy applied to "cross" men could revolutionize society. Esmerald Thorne, blameless in his professional ethics, thus appears the more deficient in his marital and parental behavior. As in the novel, Phelps reverses in heaven the roles of doctor and patient, increasing the latter's status. The most significant difference, however, is her treatment of the reunion between Helen and Esmerald: rather than creeping submissively toward her husband, Helen stands tall, lifting Esmerald to her as he begs forgiveness at her feet.

The "Gates" books offer an overview of two patterns in Phelps's work. Until the mid-1880s her central character was a woman and the books were directed to women; but beginning in mid-life, Phelps occasionally placed a man at her plot's center and argued for the reform of his behavior toward women. Her initiating this Utopian vision with an emphasis upon women's needs was more than merely personal, however. By the 1880s and 1890s human networks were at the mercy of industrial networks; women's lives were controlled by men's decisions. We must surely see Phelps's "Gates" novels as political actions. If the Utopian novel is a means of education for change, then *The Gates Between* is precisely that, its concerns being implicit in earlier "Gates" books: "The more penetrating the Utopian writer's mind is, the more clearly he understands that he is communicating a vision to his readers, not sharing a power or fantasy dream with them": such a vision Phelps communicated.[24]

Here, as in other concerns in her novels, Phelps was an innovator. As early as 1864 she began to form in her mind the Utopian suggestions of *The Gates Ajar*. Writing her next two "Gates" books in 1883 and 1887, she antedated Edward Bellamy's 1888 *Looking Backward* and the proliferation of Utopian literature during the 1890s. As often happens with work occurring at the beginning of a social movement, her books were more innovative than many that followed. She criticized conventional assumptions about gender-specific child care and housekeeping responsibilities left unquestioned by most later Utopian fiction. In 1868 she demonstrated the ineptitude of male as contrasted with female ministry. In 1883 she showed a father keeping his heavenly home while waiting the return of his earthly family. In 1887 she put a husband to work caring for his young son while awaiting his wife. Such ideas seem not to have occurred to most authors of Utopian fiction. Phelps's innovative approach to literary content (as opposed to style or structure) merits consideration in American literary history. The social criticism implicit in her heavenly city paralleled her outspoken objection to the life she saw around her. Her realistic novels of the 1870s would suggest directions that Stephen Crane, Theodore Dreiser, Charlotte Perkins Gilman, and Edith Wharton would take in their presentations of women's lives. In fact, Margaret Oliphant, reviewing *The Gates Ajar* in *Blackwood's Magazine*, found it and Bret Harte's *The Luck of Roaring Camp* (1868) to be the first worthy American successors to the works of Hawthorne and Stowe.[25]

An Established Author, 1868

The Gates Ajar thus established Phelps's literary position and made evident to her father that she must have a quiet place for writing. Eventually her father "allowed" her to adapt her mother's garden study (*Chapters*, 115). Distracted by his illness, Phelps herself led "a cramped invalid life ... quite unable to travel, scarcely ever out of Andover," as she put it. Nonetheless, her first article on women's needs—entitled "What Shall They Do?"—appeared in *Harper's New Monthly Magazine*. Here Phelps surveys the range of occupations open to women. Authorship, she notes, "is next to impossible for a woman with the care of a family on her hands": she must have "the physical strength of an Amazon and talent of the highest order." Phelps adds, "Women have died, too, in the struggle to bring the opposing forces into thorough, symmetrical union." Nor does Phelps recommend teaching and sewing which, because of overcrowding, pay low wages. Rather, she believes, women must enter a wide variety of employments, such as telegraphy, sales, or medicine. Respectability, she argues, resides not in "money or occupation" but in character. Useful occupation is, she concludes, an antidote for the unhappiness caused by a woman's "mental hunger" to live a life with an aim.[26]

Phelps followed with a second article, "Why Shall They Do It?" written for "women who can not or need not support themselves by paid employment."[27] If society censures "the unoccupied man," she writes, then "a woman should be just as much ashamed of having nothing to do." Women are not made "to play among the roses of life while their husbands and fathers are on its battle-fields," a situation "degrading to the last degree." Mothers can "spare their sons," but imprison their daughters in "maternal need and fondness." Phelps further complains that though a mother can spare a daughter "for a lifetime to be married," she can "not spare her six months to teach the freed men because [she needs] her to take care of the children!" Should genuine home need or ill health keep a widow or unmarried woman at home, Phelps relates five stories to show women how to find work near home by using their own "earnest eyes and rare invention" both to save themselves from boredom and to extend the charity beginning at home into the world about them. The article clarifies Mercy Gliddon's discussion with her mother.

In March, 1868, appeared the first story by Phelps to attract serious, as opposed to popular, literary attention. Its beginnings lay in a disaster occurring eight years earlier in Lawrence, Massachusetts, some three and a half miles from Andover. As Phelps describes it, "the Pemberton Mills, all hands being at the time on duty, without a warning of catastrophe sank to the ground. Careless inspectors had failed to note the defective core of a supporting pillar so that in time building and machinery collapsed upon 750 workers" (*Chapters*, 88-90). Eighty-eight trapped mill girls sang hymns to their deaths when a rescuer accidentally set the scene ablaze. Phelps noted that her brother Stuart, age eleven, "being of privileged sex, was sent over to the scene," but she, then sixteen, "was not allowed to go" (*Chapters*, 90-91). Some years later Phelps spent "the best part of a month" studying the tragedy. She thereby produced "The Tenth of January," published in the *Atlantic Monthly*.[28] From John Greenleaf Whittier (1807–1892) and Thomas Wentworth Higginson (1823–1911) Phelps received for this story her first literary recognition (*Chapters*, 92-93).[29]

Soon she was writing for weekly denominational papers such as the *Congregationalist* and *Watchman and Reflector*, and reviewing new books as well. Her literary reputation and literary income now established, she could turn her attention elsewhere—to women's causes. Her apprenticeship had consisted of learning to translate into female characters her feelings of alienation both from her culture and from her own potential. Her first books—the "Tiny" series—were conventional, but the second series—the "Gypsy" set—show an awakening consciousness of the constraints that growing up female placed upon a human psyche. Her own needs and experience dictated the problems of Mercy Gliddon, the *Up Hill* mill girls, Jane Gurley, and Mary Cabot. Having first attracted the attention of the reading public with a Utopian promise of women's self-fulfillment and that of the literary world with a short story of social criticism, she would spend the next twenty-years—from the 1868 publication of *The Gates Ajar* until her marriage in 1888—amplifying these two strains in her work until they overlapped. Elizabeth Stuart Phelps introduced into her realistic fiction the criticism of woman's earthly place implied by the haven for women of her heavenly vision.

Chapter Three
Exhortations to "Dream and Dare"[1]

"It is almost impossible to understand, now," wrote Elizabeth Stuart Phelps in her autobiography, "what it meant when I was twenty-five, for a young lady, reared as I was, on Andover Hill, to announce that she should forthwith approve and further the enfranchisement and elevation of her own sex. . . . Yet I do not, to this hour, like to recall, and I have no intention whatever of revealing, what it cost me" (*Chapters*, 249-50). Her body, however, would reveal the cost in increased ill health from the 1870s to the 1880s, and her characterizations of women, in spite of her intention, would indicate conflicts with which she and other women were burdened.

Such conflicts led to Phelps's difficulty in imagining characters who functioned in socially innovative roles. Their apparent inconsistent or ambivalent behavior parallels her own experience. Because Phelps's fictional women can be interpreted as psychological projections of her needs, examining her novels in their autobiographical and cultural contexts makes sense. From 1868 until her marriage in 1888 she concentrated both in essay and fiction on women and women's issues. From 1868 to 1871 she considered women's wrongs—especially double standards for sexuality and occupation; from 1871 to 1874 women's rights—namely, occupational commitment and economic self-support; from 1879 to 1886 women's pleasures—for example, a cottage "paradise" where women might function effectively in ways typically reserved for men; and from 1881 to 1886 women's needs—above all, for loving concern in a stable relationship, even though this last be available only at the price of subordination. Such considerations, as Phelps noted, "cost" her.

Women's Wrongs, 1868-1871

During this period, in both fiction and essay, Phelps emphasized concern for woman suffrage as a way to right wrongs against women, expressed indignation over the public treatment of individual women, and exposed culture-wide practices detrimental to women's welfare. The novels—*Hedged In* (1870) and *The Silent Partner* (1871)—argue against two such deeply embedded practices, namely, double sexual and occupational standards for women and for men.

Phelps's concern for women was not unique for the time: women were then organizing to obtain the rights she discussed—in 1868 by forming the New England Woman Suffrage Association, headed by Julia Ward Howe (1819-1910); and in 1870 by establishing the *Woman's Journal*, edited for its first year by Mary Ashton Livermore (1820-1905) and subsequently by Lucy Stone (1818-1893). Amid this ferment, Massachusetts governor William Claflin (1818-1905), husband of Phelps's friend Mary Bucklin Davenport Claflin (1825-1896), appointed as justices of the peace Julia Ward Howe and Mary E. Stevens, a Boston realtor. That they went unconfirmed because they were not men elicited outraged responses in the *Woman's Journal*.

Among those outraged was Phelps. In "The Gist of the Matter" she quotes a "celebrated clergyman" as saying "'Governor Claflin *has lowered himself* by appointing those women justices of the peace.'" She then wonders who had lowered himself the more, "the Governor or the reverend gentleman?"[2] The "gist of the matter," from the opponents' view as Phelps interprets it, is whether man or woman should be master. But she objects that woman has not asked to be master and wonders whether—quoting from Genesis—when God gave "'*them* dominion'" He anticipated either sex as master. Rather, she argues, the sexes must share equally the dominion of their world; and for that to be possible, "the enfranchisement of half the human race" is necessary, since "a disenfranchised race, class, sex, is a child in guardianship of and under subjection to the race, the class, the sex which administers government for and upon it."

Having recognized her social inferiority as a woman and having found that recognition reinforced by an ever-strengthening women's movement—one now legitimized by the governor of her state, who was also a personal friend—Phelps could speak more directly than in *The Gates Ajar* of wrongs suffered by women and needing correction in this world. From July, 1871 through February, 1872, she wrote fourteen articles concerning women's issues, all but one first printed in the *Independent*, and eleven reprinted in the *Woman's Journal*. In them she states crisply the views that her fictional characterizations of women also embody.

Phelps takes up one after another then-current women's problems. She notes, for example, that women's intellectual growth disappears into domestic pursuits, especially their concerns about dress; one half the world ought not to be called upon to influence the other half by its physical beauty, she warns ("Where It Goes"). She considers women's right to self-management ("Unhappy Girls") as opposed to the self-abnegation they are taught ("Too Much Conscience"). She proclaims the unhealthiness of needlework as an occupation ("The Song of the Shirt") and notes that women need means of subsistence other than marriage at a time when women exceed men by 70,000 in Massachusetts ("What They Are Doing"). Woman's monetary helplessness is enforced, she believes, by men enraptured by her beauty and unaware of the extent of their distrust of her force ("Women and Money"). Men's superior muscle—both literal and figurative—she attributes to society's expectations (and consequent training) for health and strength in men, for illness and weakness in women ("Men and Muscle"). She argues that where women appear unable to perform "masculine labor," the cause lies not in inability but in the lack of practice and the "disqualification of ignorance" ("Rights and Relatives").

In addition to considering wrongs related to material well-being, Phelps also considers more important, less tangible issues. She urges that women have a role in religion reflecting their true proportion within congregations ("'The United Head'") and that the ideal marriage be construed as a relation between a woman and man educated equally ("The New Earth"). But, Phelps believes, the great obstacle to a "New Departure" in the history of women is an "enormous dummy to which had been given the title of 'true woman'" (" 'The True Woman' "). In this last article she argues that "man's work and position are what he chooses for himself, while woman's work and position are such as he chooses for her." Woman's character, Phelps continues, has been molded of necessity, not choice, so that she is unaware of the distinction between man's direction and her destiny. And this "model of womanly excellence," she concludes, is that "most convenient to man's convenience." Finally, Phelps returns to more materialistic considerations, urging young women to refuse to bear the total burden of domestic labor and to avail themselves of other occupations; she especially recommends that they consider positions in business ("A Talk to Girls" and "A Few Words to the Girls"). The ideas in this set of articles—expressed forcefully and directly, as if supported by the depth of her being—Phelps would embody in her novels.[3]

In her second adult novel, *Hedged In* (1870), Phelps continued from *The Gates Ajar* the theme of a benefactress's power to enhance the lives of others.[4] That Phelps's six years of apprentice writing focused upon a person's need for encouragement suggests a deficit she must have felt from such circumstances as her mother's early death, her father's "feudal views" and preferential treatment of her brothers, as well as her family's inadequate recognition of her need to write. The strength of her feeling emerges from her repetitious—though ever more complex—characterizations of women who exhibit the power to nurture human growth. As in *The Gates Ajar* Winifred Forceythe strengthens Mary Cabot's self-trust after her brother's death, so in *Hedged In* Margaret Purcell nurtures Nixy Trent's capacity to pursue legitimate work after the birth of an "illegitimate" son. Thus Phelps's second theme exposes a sexual double standard which prevents a "fallen" woman from maintaining an "honest" position.

Phelps first paints with Dickensian skill the sordid Thicket Street neighborhood where Nixy, a sixteen-year-old orphan, lives when she delivers a son. If socially imposed ignorance begets the child, Phelps shows that society will impose further constraints to prevent the once-fallen from ever rising. But Nixy will not submit to the "caged" existence in a Magdalens' Home (26-27). Nor can she earn her way as waitress or domestic in order to "stay honest" (35, 41). Leaving her infant upon the doorstep of a carefully selected suburban residence, Nixy feels that "all the 'chances' closed with spring-locks when *she* drew near. The hand of every man was against her.... All the world had hedged her in" (57, 85).

The benefactress's power and the fallen woman's restricted position intersect when Nixy, like Jane Gurley, comes accidentally upon a home where "God's folks" reside (ch. 7). Margaret Purcell saves Nixy by providing five years of education that culminate in Nixy's becoming a teacher. Margaret mends in loving concern the flaws wrought by an impoverished birthright and, by expecting Nixy's social growth, makes its emergence possible. But because the ravages of an uncompromising society persist, the success Margaret achieves in Nixy can only be partial—a suggestion of what might be were society hospitable to all of its members. *Hedged In* shows Nixy denied her motherhood and her work, her health and her life. Nixy's heart pains—typically symbolic in Phelps's work of a lack of community support for an individual—cause her to resign from teaching. Subsequent free time allows her to revisit Thicket Street and to find that she can now become the benefactress of another "fallen woman," for Margaret has raised Nixy to her own morally superior state. But Nixy will not live to carry our her "Thicket Street plan" for preventing further suffering (292).

The book's conclusion, if melodramatic, provides an emblematic scene essential for conveying Phelps's message to her audience, namely, that a once-fallen woman has not irreparably sinned nor is a spotless daughter tainted in befriending her. Using conventions that her audience would have understood, Phelps marries Margaret's daughter Christina to the only eligible man in the story. Her audience would have understood the marriage to indicate the continued marital attractiveness of a woman even if her innocence has been replaced by knowledge of sexual transgression. Nixy's death in a gleaming white gown at the base of her bedroom cross would have been understood as sanctification resulting from spotless and honorable living. In Margaret, Phelps offers a new type—a model earthly parent whose loving support and nonjudgmental forgiveness would, according to Nixy, "save the world"—in effect, a female Christ (292). Daringly compassionate, though not flawless, Margaret risks an experiment to right one of the world's wrongs. Her charity, beginning at home with Christina, does not end there, but extends as well to Nixy. Each reciprocally leads the other to understand the different worlds they have come from—suburban Gower and sordid Thicket Street.

About twenty-five when she wrote *Hedged In*, Phelps still saw the nurturing woman as older, the supported woman as younger. She probably identified with Nixy, in her twenties at the end of the novel. In fact, Nixy as well as Margaret can be seen as a Christ—the latter through her loving nature enhancing others' lives, the former by succumbing to life-denying social forces. Margaret represents a living and loving Christ, Nixy a dying but victorious one. To the extent that Phelps did identify with Nixy, the character suggests symbolic suicide. In so espousing the cause of women in this novel, she may have felt that her act was as illegitimate to the "feudal" Andover she knew as would have been bearing a child out of wedlock: each act entailed disregard for the behavior typically expected of a woman and placed her outside accepted society. The fictional "fallen woman" became an objective correlative for Phelps's espousal of women's rights.

The character of benefactress became younger as Phelps herself grew older and closer to filling such a role herself. Margaret was a more complex figure than Phelps had previously created— a combination of widowed mother like Mrs. Gliddon and benefactress like Miss Granger, similar to Winifred but more revealing of her inner self. In contrast to *Hedged In*, her next novel—*The Silent Partner* (1871)—has a twenty-three-year-old benefactress, close in age to Phelps and far younger than Margaret. In fact, this benefactress, Perley Kelso, wants to become a business partner, an occupational choice Phelps recommended highly. In *Hedged In*, written before *The Gates Ajar* was published, the character closest to Phelps's emotional experience is Nixy as she struggles to overcome social constraints; in *The Silent Partner* it is Perley, confidently unyielding to the barriers she finds in her way—as Phelps became for the decade following the success of *The Gates Ajar*.[5]

Where *Hedged In* concerns the ravages of a sexual double standard, *The Silent Partner* depicts an occupational double standard that prevents a woman from exercising her inheritance as she wishes—namely, to ameliorate millworkers' lives. *The Silent Partner* contains several deaths attributable to mill conditions: a father is mangled by gears; a youth is caught in a belt; a girl, born deaf-mute to an overworked mother, crashes to her death from a flood-destroyed bridge. And that nineteenth-century wonder, the machine, sets the plot in motion by crushing in an accident the heroine's father. Perley would never otherwise have had to consider the problem for a woman of a business partnership. Her father's former partners—Mr. Hayle and his son Maverick, Perley's fiancé—are unwilling to share control with a woman and instead raise their factory manager to the partnership. What informs the Hayles's choice, Phelps implies, is male fear of female power.

But Perley circumvents the Hayles by creating her own mode of influence. Exemplifying once again the professional altruist emerging in American urban society during the 1870s, Perley voluntarily visits tenements, hears of needed services, notes omitted cultural institutions. She then proceeds to disperse her own income to establish library and schools, improve sanitation, and extend relief funds. The partnership Perley willingly eschews is marriage: "I believe I have been a silent partner long enough. If I married you, sir, [she tells the third partner], I should invest in life, and you would conduct it. I suspect that I have a preference for a business of my own" (262). Millworker Sip Garth shares Perley's position against marriage. She tells her suitor: "I've heard tell of slaves before the war that wouldn't be fathers and mothers of children to be slaves like them. . . . I won't

be the mother of a child to go and live my life over again"
(278-88). In both instances the case against marriage rests upon
the poor living conditions of millworkers: one woman would
devote her life to their improvement; the other refuses to allow
her posterity's destruction by them.

Phelps believed the refused marriage proposals to be among
the book's strengths.[6] She allows women of different social
classes the self-assurance to assume control of their own lives by
voluntarily remaining single. She shows a man's protection to be
at best a precarious security because, through accidental death, he
leaves a woman more helpless than if she had learned to support
herself from the beginning. The powerless plight of lower-class
women Phelps extends in this novel to upper-class women:
Perley is no more free than Sip to achieve her desires.

Phelps's *The Silent Partner* has attracted scholars who study
the economic, the political, and the realistic novel.[7] Without
exception, they consider her the first American novelist to treat
the theme of urban, industrial blight. Phelps attributes her concern for this issue to the influence of a short story by Rebecca
Harding Davis, "Life in the Iron Mills," appearing in the 1861
Atlantic. Davis shows how minimal living conditions thwart
artistic expression, curtail the development of affection, and
render mill labor more animal than human. Phelps in her fiction
took up each of these points. Of Davis's tale, Phelps wrote:

> That story was a distinct crisis for one young writer at the point
> where the intellect and the moral nature meet.... One could never say
> again that one did not understand. The claims of toil and suffering upon
> ease had assumed a new form.[8]

Where Davis attempted no solution, Phelps offers two possibilities, individual efforts at amelioration by both upper- and lower-
class women.

Margaret Purcell and Perley Kelso exemplify upper-class
benevolent volunteerism. Each seeks to equalize social goods
either by opening her home to unfortunate women or by dispers-
ing her wealth. Like others of her era Phelps did not question the

social and economic structures that encouraged inequality, but considered the inequality a result of failed Christianity. During this decade Phelps's language became more secular, her view less sure that upper-class effort alone was the source of a solution. As a complement to Margaret's and Perley's work, Nixy Trent and Sip Garth both plan to devote their efforts to relieving the suffering of their own class. Nixy's "Thicket Street plan" indicates Phelps's recognition that victims may know better than outsiders to their condition how best to relieve that suffering. The fictional Nixy suggests the actual case of Philadelphia prostitute Maimie Pinzer, correspondent from 1910-1922 of the "gentle" Bostonian Fanny Quincy Howe, whose help apparently rescued Pinzer and enabled her in turn to befriend young prostitutes.[9]

In these first serious adult novels Phelps insists that no victim should be punished and no heiress deprived of status rightfully inherited from her father. Such wrongs committed against women Phelps carefully analyzes so that women might blame not themselves, but their society. Her assertions were made at physical and psychic cost. At the time that *The Silent Partner* was published, the *Woman's Journal* for March 26, 1871, in a weekly column called "Concerning Women," contained an entry noting that Phelps was an invalid from "indefatigable study and a New England nervous organization" (2:12). In an 1873 letter Phelps wrote that her health collapsed after the publication of *The Silent Partner*, which she had completed in spite of her physician's objection.[10] In this letter Phelps juxtaposed topics suggestively. Of this period following the publication of *The Silent Partner*, she wrote: "I ... have been unable, beyond a little magazine or newspaper work, to use my pen since.... My life is passed like a hermit's in my study, varied by the unimportant details of a half invalid existence." She added, "Put me upon record, please, ... as warmly in sympathy with the cause of woman, and as interested especially in the struggle to compass her political rights, and industrial advancement." This passage is interesting for its direct juxtaposition of her "half invalid existence" and her "sympathy with the cause of woman." Invalidism provided Phelps with a

socially acceptable excuse for limiting any public activities to
advance "the cause of women" while enabling her to claim
nonetheless her support for this cause. In reference to herself, she
wrote to Louisa Alcott's cousin Abby W. May (1829-1888) that
"there is no death and no cure for New England nerves."[11] Such
invalidism may well have been part of that "cost" she paid for
supporting the "elevation of her sex" (*Chapters*, 250).

Women's Rights, 1872-1884

In the juvenile fiction that she published over the next decade,
Phelps would take the more positive view of showing what
women could do, namely, undertake occupations atypical for
women. This positive tone was characteristic of her juvenile
fiction until the 1890s. In addition, from 1872 to 1874 she would
emphasize two other women's issues: healthful dress and higher
education.

Throughout the spring of 1873 Phelps became involved in
dress reform. To the request of Abby May that she lecture before
the New England Women's Club (est. 1868), Phelps responded
that she might write a paper on dress reform.[12] Her thoughts on
the subject appeared in three forms: a speech delivered at the
Women's Club in April; an expansion into a four-part serial in
the *Independent* entitled "Women's Dress"; and further expansion into a book, *What to Wear?* published by June.[13] Phelps
believed that women's dress represented bad taste because (anticipating Veblen) its ostentatious cost became an advertisement
for a husband's income or a father's generosity; led to bad health
by deforming a woman's body; and produced bad morals by
rewarding a woman for the pursuit of self-adornment. Phelps
suggested that, instead, dressing rationally should be fashionable.
She considered dress reform to be on a par with extending the
ballot and opening the pulpit to women. She complained that the
"subjection of one sex by the other results in making the attrac-
tion of one the business of the other" (73); mere physical attractiveness as the basis of interest between the sexes debases both.
Dress reform became the topic of conversation in such Boston

households as Louisa May Alcott's and the subject of lively exchanges in the *Woman's Journal*.[14]

A second concern attracting Phelps's attention during 1873 was the education of women. The opening in November of a coeducational undergraduate college at Boston University provided an occasion for her to contrast it with "the 'female education' of women."[15] Sex-segregated education led, she believed, to time wasted in trying to attract the society of the other sex rather than usefully spent in preparing for wholesome intellectual competition between the sexes. Phelps favored education for women that was "human" (comparable to that training available to men), not "female" (suitable for "true women" and inferior compared to men's). She believed that the former occurred in such coeducational institutions as Cornell and Michigan. The undergraduate college of Boston University offered to women in Massachusetts the first Bachelor of Arts degree—a milestone. Its president from 1872 was ex-Governor Claflin, Phelps's personal friend. In 1876 Phelps herself was the first woman to lecture to the undergraduate students: she discussed George Eliot in a series of four lectures on "Representative Modern Fiction."[16] And in 1878 a group of women, including Phelps and her friend Mary Claflin, circulated a letter soliciting contributions to endow "a woman's professorship in Boston University."[17]

At about the time that a B.A. became available to women, opposition to their education gained strong support from Dr. Edward H. Clarke in *Sex in Education* (1873). With others, he argued that a woman's body contained only a limited amount of energy which during puberty must be untaxed to ensure sufficient development of her sexual organs. By the end of March, 1874, the *Woman's Journal* carried an advertisement for an anthology of rebuttals to Clarke, called *Sex and Education*, edited by Julia Ward Howe. Included was an essay by Phelps, presenting her previously discussed argument that women became sickly from lack of adequate stimulation and outlet for energy.[18]

While Phelps was pursuing the issues of women's health and education in speeches and articles, she also continued to write juvenile fiction. Her work of the 1870s and 1880s is less stereo-

typed than her earlier "Tiny" and "Gypsy" series, less Christian
in plot than *Mercy Gliddon, Up Hill,* or "Jane Gurley." These
later stories realistically sketch the mischievous escapades of a
four-year-old boy called "Trotty." Collected from *Our Young
Folks* into *The Trotty Book* (1870), they also reveal Phelps's
concern for women. In an 1872 letter to her publisher she
wondered whether a new selection of stories for older children
and girls might not be marketable as "Sensible Girls." But
instead, indicative of editorial estimation of public taste, a
strangely titled *Trotty's Wedding Tour, and Story-Book* appeared,
containing fourteen tales, nine of particular interest to girls, a
mutation of her desire to compile "Sensible Girls." Harder to
explain than the strange title is the fatherless state of Trotty's
family. Trotty, inspired by Phelps's youngest brother Edward
Johnson Phelps (b. 1863), is portrayed as having an older sister
Lill (Phelps was called "Lily"). When the real "Trotty" was four,
his father Austin Phelps was most surely alive. The omission
might be deference to an easily identifiable living person or
Phelps's inability ever to portray in her fiction the "tender
father" she described in her biography of him.[19]

In addition to the "Trotty" tales, Phelps wrote girls' fiction for
Our Young Folks. The early and continued encouragement of
Lucy Larcom (1824–1893), editor of the magazine, as well as a
lucrative $500 payment for restricting her juvenile contributions
during 1870 exclusively to *Our Young Folks,* kept Phelps among
that periodical's frequent contributors. In 1872 she offered the
magazine the serialization of "Our Little Woman," a story that
presented in fiction for girls two of Phelps's themes, self-support
and health. One month after the story had completed its run in
Our Young Folks, the *Woman's Journal* reprinted it. With a
sequel it appeared in book form in England as *My Cousin and I.*[20]

In the first part of *My Cousin and I,* "Our Little Woman," the
title figure Lois McQuentin vows to become a physician because
her mother, dying of cancer, wished for a woman doctor to
diagnose her disease (735). To her cousin Hannah Colby's objec-
tions to "so strong-minded" a goal, Lois replies that women make
good livings from medical practice, a point made by Phelps in an

1871 article, "What They Are Doing" (734). In addition, Lois explains her plan: she will finance high school by shoemaking and medical school by teaching (735), a regimen not less strenuous than determined women actually pursued.[21] A likely inspiration for this as well as for Phelps's adult work *Doctor Zay* (1882) was her "boon companion" of the 1870s, Dr. Mary Briggs Harris (1847–1886).

The second part of *My Cousin and I*, "Hannah Colby's Chance," considers the possibility of a woman's supporting a needy mother and being economically secure while remaining unmarried. The widowed Mrs. Colby loses her investment through a stockbroker's mismanagement in the 1873 panic. Such funds were the sole support for herself and daughters Hannah and Mary Alice. As narrator of the tale, Hannah explains:

> Mother and Mary Alice began to cry afresh, but I sat and thought. It had never occurred to me before, how much harder it was to be widows and orphans than to be widowers and orphans! Now I wondered why it was. Then I wondered why it need be.
>
> It suddenly flashed upon me that it was a very unnatural thing for three grown women (Mary Alice and I felt grown that night!) to know no more of the disposal and management of their property than we did; and a very singular thing that a man must know for us, even if he must be a man outside of the family; and rather a disgraceful thing that we should be sitting by like babies while he played with it and tossed it out of our reach. I had never thought anything about it before. (599)

Hannah determines to solve the Colby financial dilemma herself. Phelps treats as silly Mary Alice's plan to marry immediately so that her husband will support his female in-laws. Upon cousin Lois McQuentin's urging—" 'Don't teach. Don't sew. Don't. . . . You should go into business.' " (603)—Hannah first accepts an apprenticeship. As Lois points out, Hannah can work her way up in business "like a boy. It isn't being a girl that makes the difference, so much as being girl*ish*" (603). Later, Hannah and her friend Jane Betoyer set up business for themselves with a loan of "a thousand dollars at six per cent" from Hannah's brother-in-law (733). Hannah's mother decides to buy the house Jane and

Hannah rent and to take them in as boarders. This story concludes by establishing a household of women concerned with looking after each other's needs. "A home for her mother, and a woman of herself. Hannah Colby's chance has come!" crows Hannah in triumphant conclusion (740).

Phelps includes a number of issues in "Hannah Colby's Chance"—women's ignorance of finances, the non-necessity of marriage, the success of female apprenticeship, the need for dress reform, the joy of providing for one's mother, the possibility of female-managed businesses and female-financed households. Several of these themes recur in "A Brave Girl," although Phelps replaces dress reform with advocacy of women's higher education and hints the possibility of marriage.

"A Brave Girl," never appearing as a book, was serialized in the magazine *Wide Awake* from December, 1883 to August, 1884.[22] Like *Our Young Folks, Wide Awake* appealed to readers under eighteen, but, as with Louisa May Alcott's *Little Women* (1868–1869), adults as well read "A Brave Girl." In fact, John Greenleaf Whittier wrote Phelps an approving note regarding this story.[23]

The opening scene suggests the varied benefits to women of higher education. Students at Smith, the first women's college founded by a woman, discuss their future plans. The heroine, Loto Rollinstall, declares, "I shall be a Professor of Biology!" Her pal Fern Holbrook's response—"Now I never thought of it"— establishes Loto as particularly responsive to changed circumstances. The vocation of college professor was a new option: a college education had been available to women in Massachusetts only since 1873 at Boston University and after 1875 at Smith and Wellesley. Phelps, however, allows Loto an even more surprising career (at the time) for a college graduate: she successfully establishes her own business.

The condition allowing Loto to demonstrate her wage-earning capacity is her father's sudden death during her junior year. She bravely assumes Dr. Rollinstall's position as family breadwinner: "I'll look after them," she has assured him (18:174). A "brave girl," Loto sees her brother through school—not because as a male he has priority, but because as a younger sibling he is owed her support.

She also provides for her mother and herself. After trying an array of typical, low-paid, and unstable female jobs, she decides to improve her mother's idea of selling, as preserves, fruit from their own orchard. With the practical skill of the family maid and the cooperation of a grocery distributor, Loto claims, "What women have done, women *can* do" (19:95). She successfully launches the business and gains renown as the young businesswoman who has made a small fortune, educated her brother, and patented a can-cover of her own invention!

The tale concludes with Loto's speech, "Business Women," delivered to her former classmates, now Smith alumnae. Loto argues that "we make our own lives" by "wishes and duties" that are sometimes the same, and she finds that having to do that "one ... possible thing, or starve for it" might be counted a mercy (19:161). Loto's bravery consists of her accepting the same responsibilities as those of an oldest son. Although at first desiring a professorship, she inventively and intelligently establishes a successful business enterprise: the education is not lost, but put to an unanticipated use. Although the story closes with the hint that Loto may again see much of her friend Fern as a sister-in-law, its emphasis is upon Loto's business success. Phelps allows Loto to shake hands heartily with Fern's brother and return to her cans. "There is no room in this story for me to follow them," Phelps concludes. Loto's business success was worthier of note than her marital future. But by 1893, in the juvenile *Donald Marcy*, Phelps would show greater concern for male than female success.

"A Brave Girl" and "Hannah Colby's Chance," both concerning voluntary occupational commitments, are consistent with Phelps's earlier fiction in leaving marriage, typically believed to be a woman's destiny, in the background. Until 1877 the fiction contained no significant male characters. Rather, Phelps created feminine worlds into which men entered to create military or financial disaster, to question women's capacities, or to die gracefully in order that a young heroine might become a household's breadwinner. Rarely did a man offer true help to a woman, and then only to advance her own plans.

Where *Hedged In* and *The Silent Partner* show limited possibilities for women, the juvenile works show how to overcome the limitations, a pattern typical of this period where the capacity to surmount obstacles disappears from women's fiction and continues only in that for girls.[24] *My Cousin and I* and "A Brave Girl" clearly articulate Phelps's belief that women could both meet their family responsibilities (defined not as bearing infants, but as caring for sick or needful relatives) and pursue non-domestic careers. Significantly, she placed such possibilities within worlds peopled predominantly by women.

With *Hedged In* and *The Silent Partner* Phelps made radical statements regarding the legitimacy of unwed motherhood and the necessity not of marital but of voluntary occupational commitment. The emphases were psychologically sound—encouraging youth daringly to do, explaining to adults that blame lay not within themselves but in their society. In both juvenile and adult fiction Phelps offered loving encouragement to female readers in their search for personal identity.

The fiction thus far considered was written during the period when Phelps herself was asserting her independence of parental support and establishing a separate identity. She would have felt a need to be free of masculine control. Since she saw marriage in her own family subordinating women to men, she eliminated husbands from her fiction so that she might explore women's lives when freed of submission to men's wishes.

Women's Paradise, 1879–1886

One of Phelps's firm beliefs was that women should own the houses they lived in (*Chapters*, 192-94). She progressed gradually toward this goal. From the first summer she could afford it— probably 1869—Phelps escaped Andover heat for the sea breezes of Cape Ann near Gloucester, Massachusetts. Her "father's absence from Andover in search of his lost health having become a settled part of the summer programmes, [she] pursued, for a while, the career of summer boarder" (*Chapters*, 192-94). In time, she discovered secluded Wonson's Cove, and during the summer of 1876 she built herself a cottage at Eastern Point. For three summers she urged temperance reform among Gloucester fishermen, an experience she used in writing during the mid-1880s and 1890s. Of her life there, she wrote to George Eliot, "I have a tiny cottage ... where I keep old maid's Paradise while the rest of the family, who are all mountain lovers, flee to the hills. There I spend the summer with my maid, my dog, and my friends."[25] Her correspondence reveals a steady flow of visitors over the years—her brother Frank, her publisher James R. Osgood, Longfellow and his daughter, Annie and James Fields, the preacher Phillips Brooks, Boston literary critic Edwin Whipple and his wife, and Oliver Wendell Holmes, as well as her Wonson's Cove neighbors, Mary and William Claflin.[26]

The winter of 1875-1876 Phelps set herself southward. Although she had accomplished little writing that fall, the *Atlantic Monthly*, in January and February, 1876, carried her sketches about New Englanders traveling south for the winter.[27] The sketches follow the format of Louisa May Alcott's *Shawl-Straps* (1872), wherein a first-person narrator relates a mixture of fact and fiction for a reader's entertainment. Though inconsequential writing, these pieces—as well as two similar sketches appearing at about the same time in the *Independent*—constitute an early attempt at humor. In this sense they are precursors to Phelps's "Paradise" set, deriving from summer life at her Gloucester cottage.[28] In one she views with humor the life of a single woman living without masculine protection (*Old Maid's Paradise*, 1879); in the other she concocts a spoof of detective fiction to demonstrate the illusion of men's so-called protection of women (*Burglars in Paradise*, 1886). The set was reissued in a single volume as *Old Maids and Burglars in Paradise* (1887). Each was originally serialized in the *Independent* and offered in the Riverside Paper Series.[29]

In writing the "Paradise" set, Phelps joined other female humorists of the nineteenth century. In 1856 a collection of sketches by Frances Whitcher (1811–1852) called *The Widow Bedott Papers* had appeared. In the tradition of Yankee yarns, they contain a feminist character, Samanthy Hokum, whose views her creator ridicules. "Fanny Fern" (Sara Payson Willis Parton, 1811–1872) had published from 1868 to 1872 several collections of witty, satiric sketches, upon occasion deliberately pro-feminist. And Marietta Holley (1836–1926), who used the pen name "Josiah Allen's Wife," wrote twenty-one "Samantha" books from 1873 to 1914, one of which Frank Luther Mott considered a "better-seller." Although also in the tradition of Yankee humor, in contrast to Whitcher's character, Holley's Samantha took a moderately favorable view of women's rights. Phelps, however, assumed a more radical position on women's rights in her blend of Yankee humor and satiric wit.

The "Paradise" books concern the adventures of the partially autobiographical character Corona and her serving woman, Puella Virginia. The Latin sources of their names are suggestive— "Corona" of "crowned" authority and "haloed" goodness, "Puella Virginia" (meaning "girl virgin") of an unmarried maiden in need of protection; but the nickname imposed by Corona— "Puelvir," meaning "maid-man"—suggests she is Corona's servant and protector. Around these two characters Phelps creates a humorous earthly Paradise, similar to the heavenly Utopia of her "Gates" series in its combination of social criticism and Utopian experiment. For Phelps's own cottage-by-the-sea in Gloucester, Massachusetts, was her real-life feminist experiment—an experiment that she communicated to her public in sketches lacking reverence for the patriarchy legitimized by Milton's *Paradise Lost*, an important source of her imagery.

An Old Maid's Paradise shows women enjoying typically masculine pleasures, namely, building a house, heading a household, and generally enjoying the outdoors unhampered by male protection. Occurring from spring until fall, the events of *An Old Maid's Paradise* unroll from Corona's assertive words, "I want a home" (5). Clearly an unmarried woman, provided for in her married brother's household, is expected to have no wants. To her brother's suggestion that she marry, Corona responds, "I can't afford to support a husband, till the panic is over" (6).

Once established in her cottage-by-the-sea, mistress Corona and her maid Puelvir conduct a life suggestive of a married couple: the former neither knows how nor wishes to housekeep;

the latter both knows how and makes all run smoothly. For Puelvir, the life of a single woman provides her "maroon and indigo" curtains "without the plague o' Pete" and a "sight easier work, 'n better wages" than being married (77). And Corona, carefree in the company of her visiting friend Mary, enjoys a typically masculine variety of outdoor activities—rowing, fishing, and swimming; scaling cliffs, walking rocks, and purchasing a pistol.

In contrast to the pleasure-seeking of these independent women are the lives of coastal fishing folk. Corona's neighbors reveal a world in which women labor in fishnet factories, cranberry bogs, or cod-packing plants, and, worse, a world where women lose their dear ones to the ravages of the sea. Corona's upper-class "Paradise" is a frail bulwark between herself and a hostile natural environment against which the lower classes have even less protection.

A human environment of unwanted intruders poses a greater problem of defense to Corona. The cottage "Old Maid's Paradise" needs protection against the "invasion of two serpents"—the Raspberry Man, who proposes to Puelvir, and one Mr. Sinuous, who arrives to escort Mary to marriage in the city. Corona's is a "Paradise Preserved," however, for Puelvir alleges to the Raspberry Man that she had signed a ten-year contract—because, as she explains, men can never believe the simple truth of their being unwanted. Recalling with Fall's arrival that "after Paradise comes Exile," Corona and Puelvir again think of their friends and families. "For Paradise, like the Kingdom of Heaven, is within us, after all," Corona observes (195). Her dauntless self-reliance is her protection and her paradise.

In mock-heroic measure Phelps thus humorously depicts a Paradise Gained. The humor perhaps was a disguise to divert attention from behavior so iconoclastic. The laughter thus aroused might have dispelled the dismay such female capacities occasionally generated in the late nineteenth-century American public.

Although not written until seven years later, *Burglars in Paradise* (1886) continues to develop the themes and characters of *An Old Maid's Paradise*. Where the earlier book shows women safely enjoying typically masculine pleasures without masculine protection, the later shows women gulled by such protection. A spoof of detective fiction, *Burglars in Paradise* exposes the ways of man to woman. The tale opens with the return of Corona and Puelvir for their sixth summer in Paradise just after five "very dangerous men" have burglarized the cottage. The two women pass an uneasy first night. Phelps chooses to express Corona's anxiety as "a harrowing dream that she had married a minister in Montana, on a seven-hundred-dollar salary" (35).

But since no burglar appears, Corona, continuing her conquest of masculine prerogatives, successfully selects for herself a mare worth more than she has agreed to pay. Her friend Mary fears that the absence of a man will be dangerous, since Corona has secured in the cottage a bond to pay for the mare. But, after all, the presence of man-as-burglar in stealing this bond is the real cause of difficulty in Paradise.

Subsequent chapters ridicule the Fairharbor police chief, Mr. Pushett, for discovering no relevant clues; the press for its exaggerated reports; the state government for inadequate protection; and the private New York detective firm Messrs. Hide and Seek for high fees and no facts. Male relatives may inadvertently help out, but none of these gentlemen in any way secures for Corona her stolen property. An outsider to the public life of men, Phelps ridicules and exposes inherent absurdities, incongruities, and biases that she has found in these worlds of business and government. Neither, she knows, performs the services it claims to offer to the general public (i.e., women and other inferiors); rather, they operate for their mutual benefit at the public's expense.

In her private world, however, Corona faces a more dangerous sort of burglar, who appears claiming "friendship." An unnamed suitor, wanting comradeship, offers his help about the house, but Corona replies that she has "learned to do a good deal" for herself (203). Maid Puelvir receives Corona's reassurance that "the man doesn't live who could part me from you" (214). But, suggests Phelps, "by the old, old ladder of Friendship, has the most dangerous housebreaker of all climbed up to Paradise?" (220).[30]

A permanent relationship with a man—typically the goal of nineteenth-century female adulthood—Phelps consistently views not as certain to satisfy a woman but as fraught with danger for the unwary. Friendship with a man, she implies, marks for a woman the end, not the beginning, of her Paradise.

Phelps's sense of humor informed her life as well as these stories. An admirer of George Eliot, she once named a dog Daniel Deronda. In her autobiography, *Chapters from a Life* (1896), she reports overhearing from her Gloucester cottage window a little fellow asking his Mama, "Is this where the *Derondas* live?" Turning the child's error into a feminist joke, she quips, "It is the doom of women, Dan. Seven pounds of your lordly sex...orders our identity away from us!" (197)

But if identity is "ordered away," wit remains. It was always Phelps's view that *femina sapiens* should not be overlooked and that, were the world properly ordered, all women would live in Paradise. If she not surprisingly took her image of Paradise from the myth of America as a New World Garden, she made that Paradise the opposite of traditional American notions of what women want, a Paradise without male protection, without marriage, without dependence, and without innocence (the last a euphemism, after all, for ignorance).

In her fiction of the late 1870s Phelps created independent women, often emotionally tied to other women. But the need for affection—particularly a trend toward male and away from female emotional support—appears in Phelps's work during the 1880s. She permits increased participation by male characters and begins to move away from her stance of complete objection to marriage. Like *Beyond the Gates*, "A Brave Girl" suggests the possibility of marriage. The novels of the 1880s, to be discussed next—*Friends: A Duet* and *Doctor Zay*—end with the heroine's marriage. *Burglars in Paradise* suggests that this would be Corona's destiny as well. And, for the first time—in *The Gates Between*—Phelps made a male character the protagonist. The "Paradise" set (1879-1886), like the "Gates" series (1868–1887), suggests patterns of change occurring in Phelps's work as a whole.

Women's Needs, 1881-1886

Two biographical factors may have influenced Phelps's changed treatment of marriage in the 1880s. The first was her decreased contact with her friend Mary Briggs Harris, M.D., the "boon companion" with whom she shared workrooms during the late 1870s: this building located beside Austin Phelps's residence was moved in 1880 to a different location.[31] Second, Phelps's increased reliance upon nurses and doctors by this time may have led her to view marriage more favorably: bad health severely limited her own independence. Even if a woman committed herself to a vocation (as Phelps had), she would need caring friends and relatives to maintain her, should her health fail. The needs that Phelps's earlier fiction emphasizes progress in accordance with psychological theory: a person's bodily needs must be satisfied before self-fulfillment can occur. Occupation may furnish material needs, but only other people can provide the security, love, and respect necessary to attaining a self-fulfilling existence. Women support each other in Phelps's early fiction. But the work published during the 1880s showed the need for emotional support leading a woman to accept against her better judgment marriage to a partner socialized to "imperious" behavior—"imperious" being Phelps's derogatory epithet for man's dominance over woman. Apparently, by the 1880s, Phelps allowed only younger women the emotional support of another woman ("A Brave Girl"); an older woman must find a man (*Beyond the Gates*), but as friend to a woman, he might be "the most dangerous housebreaker of all" (*Burglars in Paradise*).

In a letter to William Dean Howells, written March 10, 1880, Phelps discussed her intent in the recently completed work, *Friends: A Duet* (1881), to make her readers feel

sadness at my heroine's acception of anything below the highest in the marriage relation.... [She] is beset by the refined moral problems arising out of the faithful friendship of a truly noble man.

The light-natured reader will be glad she married him. The other kind will almost wish she had not.[32]

By 1880 Massachusetts had significantly more women than men—a differential, more apparent in urban than in rural areas, which eliminated for some women the pursuit of marriage and motherhood. Thus, in her fictional dissection of courtship from a woman's viewpoint, Phelps legitimizes for single women their deviation from tradition. Superficially the novel met popular expectations, but most of its pages would lead a thoughtful reader to question the very solution it offers—a resolution meeting a man's rather than a woman's needs.

In *Friends*, Phelps's protagonist, Reliance Strong, offers a variation on the benefactress role. As with Winifred Forceythe, Reliance's "heavenly marriage" exists outside of the novel. Widowhood has left her free to devote herself to philanthropy: being needed by the needy removes the loneliness resulting from her husband's death. Reliance's concern is not her parlor maid, as in Phelps's work of the 1860s and 1870s, but her parlormaid's alcoholic father. Reliance believes that one day someone would "do for these poor slaves to drink what Harriet Stowe did for the black ones" (126), a comment foreshadowing Phelps's *A Singular Life* (1895). *Friends* contains her first fictional use of the temperance reform she had attempted. In considering alcoholism, she emphasizes changing masculine behavior to meet more adequately women's and children's needs.

Phelps's consideration of courtship and marriage in this novel shows how far short of her ideal masculine behavior falls. In February, 1874, Phelps had published in the *Independent* a piece called "A Dream within a Dream"—concerning her ideal for marriage, which eliminates all subordination of woman to man. Each spouse is to be faithful, to "reverence" the other, and to resist the claim of one to "legislate" for the other.[33] But the pattern of male-female interaction emerging from the courtship "duet" between Reliance and her husband's friend Charles Nordhull in *Friends* shows his increasing imperiousness toward her. Charles, articulating his desire for friendship in an easy "imperious" way, begins to feel a "thrill of pride akin to the haughtiness of possession" (95-99).

In counterpoint to the progress toward Charles's possession of
Reliance, Reliance and Charles agree that "if a rational man and
woman in a rational state of society cannot pursue a rational
friendship without contemplating or perpetuating a marriage
engagement, either by accident or design, then civilization is a
failure" (157). Phelps understands the dynamics of human interactions in noting the power of expectations to shape the development of a relationship and the consequent difficulty of trying to
live within a relationship for which no social code exists. Marriage, simply by its existence and by others' assumption of its
emergence, exerts pressure against the success of Reliance and
Charles in maintaining an alternative—a dreary prognosis from
a woman who expressed a woman's right to control her life as
articulately as Phelps did.

Friends presents marriage as an institution desired by the man
but merely tolerated by the woman. In contrast to "silent
partner" Perley Kelso, Reliance must relinquish rather than
retain her own desire for friendship in favor of Charles's for
marriage. Reliance goes to bed in surrender to her anxiety. Her
illness expresses the conflict with which her consciousness cannot cope. Although not desiring to marry, she nonetheless prefers living a shared life.

Charles feels that "it was as if four of them were there—John
and Reliance Strong, Charles Nordhull and Charles Nordhull's
vision [of his ideal self]" (109)—a concrete acknowledgment of
the psychological contamination inherent in past experience and
future hope. In a culture where a man expects his wife to serve
him, where a wife expects to be a man's "idol upon a pedestal,"
Charles underestimates the strength of character required to go
against behavioral norms (228). Rather than having undergone a
changed view in refusing Reliance her desire and in requiring her
subordination to Charles's "imperious" needs, Phelps with
relentless realism depicts the pressures that a man could successfully exert upon a woman to satisfy his own wishes. Phelps closes
the novel: "It was heaven on earth, at least, to him. If to her it was
earth after heaven, what cared he?" (255)

Society offers Reliance only one legitimate possibility for a "shared life" with a man—submission to the "bondage" of institutionalized marriage (216, 218). In a world Phelps believes to have gone awry, women and men must relate to each other according to limited prescriptions, to women's disadvantage. Charles once remarks, "Somebody must care enough—for most of us—to hold us up, each in our different ways. . . . It ought to make us all patient with one another" (49). Such mutually supportive patience as Charles mentions, a social characteristic important to Mary in *Beyond the Gates,* is neither expected nor rewarded by the world which Reliance and Charles inhabit—a world as close as fiction could make it to Phelps's own.

In contrast to the uncompromising realism of *Friends, Doctor Zay* (1882), a more idealistic work, suggests—but does not show—the possibility of married happiness for a woman committed to a career.[34] Doctor Zaidee Atalanta Lloyd—orphan of a wealthy Maine doctor and fatally ill mother, whose name she "wore"—maintains a successful country practice specializing in the care of women and children. Phelps wrote to Howells (November 2, 1881) that she knew such professional women "thoroughly from long personal observation under unusual opportunities."[35]

Following her pattern of the 1880s, Phelps de-emphasizes relationships between women here. The patient whose convalescence the novel records is not a woman or a child—the patients Zay claims to desire—but a man, one Waldo Yorke, visiting to look after inherited property. As the physician attending Yorke after a carriage accident, Zay exhibits characteristics typically associated with men—professional competence, expectation of obedience from subordinates, and superior horsemanship. Yorke becomes as dependent upon Zay as female patients upon competent male physicians. To Yorke's confession that he loves her, Zay responds that he is "only nervous," such "love" being symptomatic of patient-physician dependence (191, 198). Zay's behavior is a near-caricature of the treatment of female patients by nineteenth-century male physicians.

Phelps develops Yorke's love for Zay gradually, but hers for him appears suddenly in the next to last chapter. Like most of Phelps's men who love women, Yorke becomes "imperious"—glorying in haughty self-possession, their roles now reversed. Like Reliance, Zay finds it "a fearful thing for a woman to love a man." Phelps suggests in novel after novel that the "natural" way for a woman to love is through self-effacement, for a man through domination; consequently, her women fear heterosexual love.

In Zay, Phelps creates a new woman whom marriage would be less able to subordinate because of her already well-established commitment to a career; in Yorke, she attempts a "new type of man" who by supporting a woman's career eliminates her having to choose between occupational self-fulfillment and devoted companionship. Strategically, she concentrates upon Yorke's view for Zay, nearly to the exclusion of Zay's own viewpoint—perhaps to suggest the attractiveness of a professional woman as wife. But for all Phelps's optimism regarding women's medical competence, she was as ambivalent regarding a woman's capacity to maintain her independence in marriage as she had been in *Friends*—unless a "miracle" should occur (247). The novel stops before readers reach the brink of the miraculous—a married Zay continuing her practice with no loss of Yorke's happiness.

Other fictional treatments of the woman as physician appeared during the 1880s: Howells's *Dr. Breen's Practice* (1881) and Sarah Orne Jewett's *A Country Doctor* (1884). Phelps found Howells's Dr. Breen an unfair example of a professional woman, since Howells allows Dr. Breen a practice of one patient, quickly relinquished to a male physician, and indicates that she obtained medical training only to compensate for disappointment in love. Such a portrait Phelps—as well as Alice Stone Blackwell of the *Woman's Journal*—could only scorn. Jewett, on the other hand, created in Nan Prince a woman who considers the business of healing her duty. Blackwell applauded Jewett's requiring Nan to choose career over marriage. But Jewett concludes her story before Nan establishes a successful practice. Of these three fictional physicians, Phelps's Dr. Zay is the most innovative characterization—that least congruent with current stereotypes.[36]

Brief Parallels: Short Fiction of Two Decades

An overview of Phelps's short stories of two decades charts her changing themes, not surprisingly parallel to or foreshadowing her book-length fiction. She collected ten stories in *Men, Women, and Ghosts* (1869).[37] Between 1865 and 1868 all but one had appeared in *Hours at Home, Harper's New Monthly*, or the *Atlantic*. Half these stories focus upon relations between the sexes. (More than three quarters of her uncollected stories end with the obligatory marriage. These in general are stereotyped in characterization and undistinguished in execution.) Several from *Men, Women, and Ghosts* merit note as they foreshadow later work. "The Tenth of January," previously mentioned, had elicited her first literary recognition and suggests *The Silent Partner*. "One of the Elect" (first published as "Magdalene") foreshadows *Hedged In* in treating sympathetically a woman considered to be a social pariah. "Night-Watches"—the amusing monologue of an author about her difficulties resulting from insomnia—looks to the humorous tone of *An Old Maid's Paradise*. And in "No News" Phelps begins to articulate the trials for a woman of marriage and maternity, a theme central to *The Story of Avis* (1877). Two uncollected stories, "Margaret Bronson" (*Harper's New Monthly*, 1865) and "An Hour with Gwendolyn" (*Sunday Afternoon*, 1879), also deserve mention. The heroine in the former, a "strong-minded" woman, still single by her own wish, saves the life of a Civil War soldier by the accuracy with which she handles a pistol. Battlefire does not daunt her; nonstereotypic bravery makes her attractive to a prospective lover just as Zay's competence in the later novel attracts a man to her. The latter story debates the interpretation of Gwendolyn Harleth from George Eliot's *Daniel Deronda* (1876). None of these stories is stylistically meritorious. Their interest lies in hinting at socially iconoclastic roles for women that Phelps would later develop in greater detail.

During the decade of the 1870s Phelps moved beyond considerations of marriage and heterosexual relations to depict a range
of institutions and relationships. The majority of stories from
this period depict characters apart from marital concerns. In
Sealed Orders (1880) Phelps collected seventeen stories—three
previously appearing in the family-oriented *Hearth and Home*
and *Golden Rule*, and the rest in the *Atlantic, Scribner's,
Harper's New Monthly*, and the *Independent*.

Several stories in this collection continue to depict the effect of
poverty on women's lives, a theme central to *Hedged In* and *The
Silent Partner*. "The Lady of Shalott" depicts drink, piecework,
and unsanitary slum conditions as villains in the lives of two
sisters. "Old Mother Goose," like *Hedged In*, shows that "The
world is so hard on women" who bear a child out of wedlock.
Even if that child becomes a renowned actress, her name still
"will not bear the scorch" of her mother (46). "Doherty," a
drunken vagrant who finds relief in being imprisoned, owns the
voice of a singer, but her environment provides little outlet for
such talent.

The themes of *Friends* and *Doctor Zay* had previously
appeared in short fiction. Two stories—"Running the Risk" and
"Miss Mildred's Friend"—consider the different expectations
women and men bring to a relationship. In the former story the
woman finally sets aside her love for a man killed in a railroad
wreck to marry another man—but only after he is permanently
disabled in a fire. Expectations that she be true to a deceased lover
prevent her recognizing a new love. The second story depicts a
woman who desires friendship where the man wants marriage.
But unlike *Friends*, Phelps permits the woman to prevail. A third
story, not appearing in *Sealed Orders* but worth noting for its
depiction of a woman as physician, is "Zerviah Hope" (*Scribner's*
1880)—entitled not for its heroine but for her male nurse. The
physician foreshadows Dr. Zay in character and competence. She
and her male nurse work as an empathetic team, but he dies in an
epidemic leaving the physician bereft of companion and aide. As
in *Zay*, Phelps inverts the typical pattern of male dominance.

Another group of stories foreshadows *A Singular Life* of 1895.
Several show the influence of Phelps's Gloucester summers:

"Wrecked in Port," "Sealed Orders," and "The Voyage of the *America*" depict the hardships and uncertainties of sea life. Other aspects of *A Singular Life* developed in stories of the 1870s include the home mission in "A Woman's Pulpit," the alcoholism in "Neblitt," and the anticlerical stance in "Saint Caligula."

Stories of this decade show Phelps's increased control over realistic detail. More than a third use a first-person viewpoint to advantage, either as a framing device or as a participant observer. Phelps relies less upon the stereotypic conclusion of marriage, actual or implied, and instead death, illness, or other loss ends many tales. Just as in her juvenile work Phelps moved from the sentimental Christian emphasis of the "Tiny" series to the real-life need of earning a livelihood as in "Hannah Colby's Chance," so in her stories she relied less upon typical, more upon innovative content in later work.

Life's Losses

Disapproval and death punctuate the 1880s. Anti-women's-rights essays by her father plus deaths of brother and friend left a vacuum in Phelps's life by mid-decade.

Clear evidence of unacceptability to Phelps's father of her beliefs about women exists in two essays. In the first, "Woman-Suffrage as Judged by the Working of Negro-Suffrage" (1878), Austin Phelps ridicules the results of freedmen's efforts at self-government and urges the error of enfranchising those unable "even to understand" the ballot (96). In addition, he points out, suffrage should extend only to those having the "physical" power to defend it; women of course lacked such (98). In both cases he found suffrage to be "legislation *against nature*" (103). The essay shows a blend of misogyny and idolization of women, two sides of the same pattern: adore the woman who fits one's rigid standard, revile her who does not. Reprinted in the *Woman's Journal,* the essay received unequivocal rebuttal from editors Lucy Stone and her husband Henry Blackwell.[38]

The second essay, "Reform in the Political Status of Women" (1881), more blatantly undercut his daughter's concern for the rights of women. She had noted publicly and privately that she

shared J. S. Mill's views in *The Subjection of Women,* but her
father considered the essay to have fostered "antagonism...bet-
ween the sexes."[39] He declared,

Once fill a young woman's mind with the notion that it is a grander
thing to be a speaker on the platform than to be a wife in a Christian
home, that it is a nobler distinction to be a successful author than to be
the happy mother of children, that it is more honorable to head a
half-score of "committees" for public service than it is to be a loving
daughter in a father's house, the model of refinement to younger
brothers and sisters, and you can no longer find a place of honor in her
thoughts for the mission of either daughter, wife, or mother. (110-11).

He did concede at the end of this essay that "conservative and
Christian men" might support "the higher education of women,
the extension of the range of their employments without loss of
caste, their protection from swindlers in their tenure of property,
and the extension of their usefulness in organized charities"
(116). Contrary to her father's belief that improvements best
"take the type, not of reform, but of development, not of revolution, but of growth"(116), the daughter had publicly spoken of
humanitarian "revolution" and the economic self-support to
effect it.

The appearance of *Beyond the Gates* in 1883 coincided with
the accidental death of Phelps's gifted brother Stuart. On August
29 he tripped over his loaded gun as he entered a canoe in woods
near Bar Harbor, the locale where Austin Phelps had been
summering for some years. Stuart possessed unusual intellectual
abilities and was an inspired teacher, according to President
Seelye of Smith College, where he had been Professor of Mental
and Moral Philosophy since the fall of 1878. Stuart had also
lectured in psychology at Andover Seminary during the academic
year 1881–1882, a fact that may account for Phelps acknowledging that the pages of *Beyond the Gates* owed "more to his
criticism" than she could indicate. (She, however, earlier had
influenced Stuart's choice of discipline.) Friends and relatives
expected that Stuart's death would cause the death of his invalid

father. But, noted the daughter, "To the amazement of us all, his health after that August day did not immediately or rapidly decline. On the contrary, it might even be said that he gained." Undervaluing himself as he did because of the great contrast between his excessively high ideals for himself and his severe underestimation of his own self-worth, Austin Phelps apparently accepted Stuart's death as the relief of just punishment for his own failure to achieve these ideals—hence his apparent "gain" in health.[40]

Phelps's letters reveal the impact upon her of Stuart's death. First, not only must she deal with her own shock, but her family—particularly her invalid father—required her ministrations. Second, her writing ceased: not until the following January did she submit any new work. Third, by February, 1884, she suffered the "first acute illness since her childhood" and found herself unable to leave Andover. And fourth, she lost contact with her literary support group. She had, she claimed, suffered a long decline since the shock of her brother's death: Stuart was "exceptionally near to [her]," the dearest to her of all save her father.[41] Trained as she had been to depend upon male authority, once more, as in the loss of Thompson, she found an important source of such support removed. Not until *Burglars in Paradise,* begun in November, 1885, did she again write a book-length work.

No sooner was that work in progress than another death impinged upon Phelps's life. Mary Briggs Harris died suddenly of incurable heart disease in 1886. If it was important for a woman to have the support of a close friend who was a woman and to have access to a physician who was a woman, then in losing Harris, Phelps was doubly deprived. Never after 1886 did she imagine women having the energy and stature of her earlier characters. As the death of Thompson can be seen to have terminated expectations of ever leading the life of a conventional wife and mother, so the death of Harris ended Phelps's period of directly expressing her "love for women."

After this she apparently could no longer exhort women to "dream and dare." Less insecure than she had been during the 1860s, during the 1870s she was more congruent in her beliefs and activities, more secure in her sense of self than she would ever be again. The direction of support between younger and older women had become reversed in Phelps's fiction, as in her life. From her mid-twenties until her mid-thirties, she was periodically able to deal with those issues of deepest concern to her—although not without bodily distress. Her strong complaints about the wrongs done to women by sexual and occupational double standards, her exhortations to young women to claim their rights to work, her semi-autobiographical, humorous demonstrations of the pleasures and strengths of single womanhood—these are works that authentically portray her point of view. But beginning in the 1880s, after a second bout of illness following the completion of a novel, after her father's anti-suffrage essays, after she ceased to share rooms with Harris, her novels began to treat marriage as if inevitable. The marriages do not exemplify the requirements of her ideal for marriage, nor are they consistent with the woman's desire to remain free of the bondage that marriage causes her. Since such marriages clearly do not fit Phelp's marital values, they must suggest the desires of either public or editor, or her own estimation of how little control of their lives women could expect to exert. That both Reliance Strong and Atalanta Zaidee Lloyd are overcome by their suitors is less a statement of their preference than of their being finally ground down. So also was Phelps, but with a difference. Her own effort was divided between her worship of a family patriarch, whose authority she had been taught from childhood to respect, and her allegiance to women as a group, which the examples of women from her youth and the early women's rights movement encouraged. Perhaps the deepening of this conflict, as much as any other biographical factor, accounts for the marked contrast between her fictional women of the 1860s, 1870s, and early 1880s, and those that would emerge by the 1890s.

Chapter Four
Her "Favorite Heroine" and "Dearest Hero"[1]

In 1903, after fifteen years of married life, Elizabeth Stuart Phelps wrote to Harriet Prescott Spofford (1835–1921), a widowed Massachusetts author, "Marriage is such tremendous material for the novel writer! I wonder that it is not worn out in the using."[2] Phelps found the marriage relation "tremendous material" because in depicting the interactions between individual women and men she could demonstrate what each expected of, or was willing to allow in, the other. Phelps's depiction of marriage, often central in her fiction, changed over time as did her own marital status. The contrast between the main characters of *The Story of Avis* (1877) and *A Singular Life* (1895) is particularly revealing.

In the 1903 letter to Spofford, Phelps observed that "the married are hampered in what they can say. I remember that when I wrote *Avis* I said 'were I married, I could not write this book.'" Her fiction followed her living. Deaths among friends and relatives likely led to her giving up her single status, a fact that in turn shaped the writing. Once married, her focus changed. In addition, her mother's fiction implied a critique of marriage that influenced Phelps's work. Thus her life, including her mother's fiction, provides the necessary context for understanding the novels containing her favorite characters.

Chapters from her Life:
The Autobiography and Friendships

During the 1860s and 1870s, Phelps's writing indicated her preference for an independent life, but so atypical a choice, to be workable, would have needed strong support from those around her—family, of course, but also friends. Her autobiographical reticence makes assessment difficult, however. Its title deriving from that of an autobiographical novel by her mother, the serialization of Phelps's autobiography *Chapters from a Life* began in the December, 1895, issue of *McClure's Magazine,* a periodical having a wide circulation.[3] Phelps discusses her early life (chaps. 1-3), her early writing (chaps. 4-6), her professional life (chaps. 7-9, 11), her individual concerns (chaps. 10-11), and her literary creed (chap. 12). The work is not narrative but thematic in organization. Its focus is the career, not the woman. It exhibits the same stylistic contortions evident throughout most of Phelps's work.

Unlike the more conservative book version, the serialization contains several revealingly captioned photographs. For example, although the book makes no reference to Lt. Samuel Hopkins Thompson (her undeclared suitor), the serialization includes his class photograph, locates him in it, and identifies his father. In referring directly only to deceased relatives and to friends having public stature, she followed current good taste; as a proper "true woman," she did not reveal intimacies and confidences from either her own or others' private lives. In addition to following proper decorum, such a strategy of concealment would have protected a retiring woman whose work forced her into the public's consciousness. She presented herself in the public roles of author and reformer; her private life she largely concealed. She was an uncertain autobiographer as she navigated the "untried coast" of yet another genre (*Chapters,* 2). That she began her *Chapters* by grounding herself in the detail of her regional Gloucester surroundings is no accident, since Gloucester was also the setting of her best fiction.

Her approach to the project—as if she were charting an "untried coast"—emphasizes the self-doubt and uncertainty with which, save for one generous decade, she approached so much of her writing and living. She still acknowledged her sympathy with the cause of woman, placing it second only after her belief in "Life Everlasting" (*Chapters,* 250). As additional tenets of her creed she listed the "abolition of liquor traffic," anti-vivisection (a cause which she began to espouse about 1895, but which entered a

novel only in 1904), modernization of the legal system, and the
"homeopathic system of therapeutics" (*Chapters,* 251-52). The
last paragraphs of the book express her hope that she has
recounted those lessons from her life most "educative" to herself,
and therefore most likely to make the lives of her readers "easier
to live" and "more possible to live happily" (278). Finally, she
observes that, like an unnamed autobiographer, perhaps she too
"'had concealed [her]self behind an autobiography'"—a view
with which her contemporary, the critic Lilian Whiting, concurred.[4]

Chapters from a Life was an image created for public consumption. Phelps's omissions are many. Still living, her second stepmother and three younger brothers are unmentioned. Nor does
the text include any mention of her undeclared suitor. Also
omitted are Andover girlhood friends such as Agnes Park; the
idol of Phelps's youthful devotion Gail Hamilton (pseudonym for
Mary Abigail Dodge, 1838-1896); her "boon companion" Mary
Briggs Harris; and the various women who had served her as
maids and to whom she would inscribe a 1901 novel, *The Successors of Mary the First.*

Phelps's arrangement of the literary figures that she included
progresses from those of international to those of regional
renown. The first chapter on the subject (chap. 7) treats Harriet
Beecher Stowe and Annie and James T. Fields. Apparently she
viewed them as her most eminent acquaintances. All had attained
international stature—Stowe through *Uncle Tom's Cabin,* James
Fields as partner in Ticknor and Fields (the American publisher
of British and Continental authors), and Annie Fields as James's
brilliant literary hostess. (Correspondence indicates that Phelps
met Sarah Orne Jewett at the Fields's home.)[5] A second chapter
(chap. 8) concerns her friendships with the nationally acclaimed
poets Henry Wadsworth Longfellow, John Greenleaf Whittier,
and Oliver Wendell Holmes—each old enough to have been her
father. A third chapter (chap. 9) discusses members of the
Greater Boston intellectual scene—Celia Thaxter, poet from
New Hampshire; Lucy Larcom, editor and writer from Massachusetts; Lydia Maria Child, abolitionist and journalist from New
England; and Phillips Brooks, reform minister from Boston's
Trinity Church. In the chapter following her discussion of her

Gloucester years Phelps considers the relatively unknown but empathetic poet Edward Rowland Sill (chap. 11). With the exception of a footnoted reference to Mary B. D. Claflin, recently deceased author and reformer, Phelps reveals relationships with no other friends.

Much less autobiographical commentary and far fewer letters exist regarding Phelps's friendships with women than with men. Since her female friends were typically closer in age to herself than her male friends, they were still living in 1896 and, as noted, decorum forbade her writing about them. In addition, since her autobiography was written for a popular serial, she may have gauged her commentary to meet what she (or her publisher) estimated to be the public's demand for information—the more notable the friend, the more pages the audience would be interested in reading. In the 1903 letter to Spofford, Phelps indicated her desire to destroy her correspondence. She wrote that she was "'calling in' ... letters from everywhere, at this time" as fast as she could and that "the first step in preparation for another world consists in the annihilation of the letters written in this!"[6] Although this letter appears to be the only indication that Spofford and Phelps were acquainted, it seems likely, given its content, that they knew each other better than the lack of evidence would suggest. Spofford was, of course, very much alive in 1896 and so does not appear in *Chapters*.

Although Phelps claimed to be a frequent guest in Boston parlors, she also spent many solitary invalid hours in Andover—hours that provided her ample opportunity to crave friends' approval for herself and her work. No evidence exists, however, that she was emotionally close to any of the women discussed. Their friendly interest in her and her work would have been encouraging, but could not have provided the quality of support a single woman might require.

Burglary of Paradise: Her Marriage

To maintain her unmarried status in a society valuing the married, Phelps would have needed friends or relatives emotion-

ally closer to her than was the case by the mid-1880s. Her favorite
brother had died. Of the remaining three, only one still lived in
Andover by 1888 when her father's condition worsened seriously.
Of her mother's sisters, only Sarah Stuart Robbins (1817-1910)
of Newton remained alive. Among friends, Harriet Beecher
Stowe had long ago moved away. Lydia Maria Child, Celia Thaxter, and Lucy Larcom were not intimate friends. Her "boon
companion" Dr. Mary Briggs Harris had died. Mary Claflin,
though friend and Gloucester neighbor, had the distractions of
spouse and children. Annie Fields had been a closer friend of
Jewett than of Phelps since James Fields's 1881 death. Longfellow had died, and Whittier and Holmes, though friends, were not
Phelps's intimates, while Sill, who might have been, died young.[7]

Not surprisingly, Phelps turned her thoughts toward the possibility of marriage. She accepted as a partner Herbert Dickinson
Ward (1861-1932), seventeen years her junior, an aspiring, but
sickly, journalist. A careful reader of Phelps's work would recognize her precedents. Four years before her 1888 marriage Phelps
discussed with understanding approval the marriage to younger
men of Germaine de Staël, Margaret Fuller, Charlotte Brontë,
and George Eliot. These women seemed thereby to have managed egalitarian relationships.[8] As early as 1885 in a letter to
Ward's father—William Hayes Ward, editor of the *Independent*—
Phelps had observed that she was "so much older."[9] Her reference to age as a problem suggests that she already looked more
seriously ahead to a "burglary" of her single "paradise."

Phelps had known her future husband's family from his childhood. Like Phelps a motherless child, Ward was raised by his
father and two aunts. Ward completed his secondary education at
Phillips Academy in 1880, graduated from Amherst in 1884, then
taught for a year in North Carolina. He studied theology for two
years at Union Theological Seminary (1885-1887) and a final
academic year at Andover, ending in June, 1888. He is described
as having been a man of "unusual cultivation and markedly
original views"—apparently attractive to a woman whose conversation was noted for its captivating brilliance and "magnetic
power."[10]

Fortunately, several letters from Phelps to Ward's father and aunt remain to document the development of their relationship. At first, Phelps appears to have taken an interest in Ward simply because he was the son of a long-standing acquaintance. Her first extant mention of him occurred in a letter to his father written from Gloucester, in August, 1884. She indicated that she liked his "boy" and found him a "fine fellow" in whom his father might "take a world of comfort." A year later, in October, 1885—upon W. H. Ward's return from a yearlong archeological expedition— Phelps wrote that his "boy" interested her and she wished to "do more for him"; to this end she wished to pose a question. In a subsequent letter she explained that her "question concerned his religious position"; she wished to be remembered to him and offered the reminder that she expected the promised letters.[11]

The friendship progressed. On December 17, 1885, feeling "too ill" to take the train, Phelps had become sufficiently close to Ward that she might send him in her stead to Whittier with a birthday remembrance. This note to Whittier requested that if Mrs. Claflin were present, he introduce Ward as a "great friend" of hers. Whittier's response, written December 20, suggested that in fact a courtship was in progress, for he wrote, "Give Mr. Ward my warm congratulations. God bless you both! He has blest you in bringing you together."[12]

Concurrent with the developing relationship, however, was Phelps's markedly poor health. In 1886 she disabled her hand; in 1887 she lost the use of her eyes, suffered a sprained back and ankle. A year later, in April, 1888, when she and Ward planned to visit Whittier together, her eyesight still bothered her. Nor was Ward healthy. In May, 1888, Phelps wished to talk over with W. H. Ward his son's plans: she wanted young Ward to have the health she felt he needed to fulfill the teaching post he had obtained in Alabama.[13]

Between late spring and early fall of 1888 Phelps wrote Ward's aunt, Hetta Hayes Ward, a series of letters that define her own expectations for herself and young Ward. In the first of six extant letters Phelps undertook to practice the role of successful woman healer as she had developed it in *Doctor Zay* (1882), an instance of fiction instructing life. Subsequent letters express excessive concern for Ward's safety upon various sailing cruises. For example, on July 28 Phelps wrote "Miss Hetta" that she shared her anxiety about the cruise and had taken the precaution of privately placing life-savers aboard. Phelps still occasionally referred to Ward as "the boy"—surely a parental, rather than marital, mode of reference. Other letters show her sharing information regarding Ward's accomplishments. For example, July 30, Phelps wrote "Miss Hetta" that "Herbert spoke last night...to a crowded house.... He did finely. I was more than pleased. It was a perfect success. He went off [on his cruise] very tired; but happy, I thought."[14] But, for reasons best known to themselves, Phelps did not reveal to Ward's aunt any plans they may have had regarding a common future.

On October 20, 1888, Phelps's brother, the Reverend Lawrence Phelps, assisted by Ward's father, officiated at her marriage in Gloucester to young Ward. Only a few members of the respective families were present; Austin Phelps, in Bar Harbor, was not among them. A note to Whittier three days later announced the marriage—"You cannot be more astonished than I am—but I am happy"—and offered their "terror of the newspapers" as the reason for their secrecy.[15] Phelps and Ward then visited their respective families before traveling to Summerville, South Carolina, where they wintered.

Phelps reports in a letter to Whittier that she finds Ward "a very good husband—far better than ... deserved or expected" and then adds, "Marriage is a curious lesson! We are turning our first leaf tenderly and philosophically, too." She quips, "Eden is much improved by a good cook. I brought my devoted Northern maid with us. And she is almost as happy as we. Who was it? George Meredith? who said: 'Kissing don't last, *cookery do*!'" However, her eyes again bothered her.[16]

During the first three years of marriage they wrote together two unsuccessful biblical romances—*The Master of the Magicians* (1890), treating the story of Daniel, and *Come Forth* (1891), the story of Lazarus. Both are unreadable attempts to popularize recent Oriental scholarship. Literary collaboration failing, Phelps seems to have functioned as advocate for Ward's writing and nurse to his ill health. What she received from him is less clear. In *Chapters,* she claimed, "I cannot express in these few words the debt which I am proud to acknowledge to him who has never hindered my life's work by one hour of anything less than loyal delight in it, and who has never failed to urge me to my best, of which his ideal is higher than my own" (243). But in the 1903 letter to Spofford Phelps despaired that she had tried by turns love and faith and tact, and all three—unsuccessfully.[17] Eventually they wintered apart, Ward seeking Southern warmth, Phelps remaining in Massachusetts.

Her probable need for companionship had thus led her into a marriage of uncertain reward. But her fiction of the 1870s and early 1880s—as well as her mother's fiction before her—had anticipated the problem. Previously, in *The Story of Avis* (1877), Phelps had shown marriage eclipsing a woman artist's creativity. This view came not from her own but from her mother's experience and writing. Her mother over time in her fiction had paid increasingly serious attention to a woman's need to pursue self-fulfilling activity and had recognized that her domestic responsibilities thwarted such achievement. *The Sunny Side; or, The Country Minister's Wife* (1851) advocates an informal program of daily reading and writing for an adult woman plus formal education for a young woman. *The Angel Over the Right Shoulder* (1852) exposes the enthralling nature of domestic responsibility and a mother's apprehension regarding her daughter's future. "The Husband of a Blue" in *The Tell-Tale: or Home Secrets Told by Old Travelers* (1853) insists upon a woman's passion for writing, a career open to her without training. In *The Story of Avis* the daughter Phelps demonstrates a woman's capacity for successful professional training, and thereby expands her mother's literary legacy—an implied critique of woman's sphere.[18]

Phelps recasts her mother's living and writing into a critique of what was and a suggestion of what might be. Women's needs, sometimes presented with ambivalence by the mother, received unqualified support from the daughter. In fiction as in life,

Phelps shows, the world's expectations, not a woman's nature, hedged her in.

"Tremendous Material": Her Fiction

Assuming that Phelps's mature work began in 1870 with *Hedged In,* we need now survey her fictional marriages through 1895, when she wrote *A Singular Life.* Phelps's thinking about marriage, the "tremendous material," falls into three periods: (1) in that written before 1877, female protagonists refuse marriage; (2) from 1877 through 1886, they accept marriage, but with unfortunate or ambiguous results; and (3) from 1887 onward, male protagonists expect emotional support from women in marriage. To a great extent, biographical circumstances influenced this progression. The contrast between the central characters of *The Story of Avis* and *A Singular Life*—particularly as each experienced marriage—derives from the ambivalence that burdened Phelps's living. Like her invalidism, the characters are manifestations of inner conflict—what she called the "civil war" of a woman's dual nature (*Chapters,* 12; *Avis,* 192). Her "favorite heroine" is closely associated with her understanding of her mother's life; her "dearest hero," her father's life. That her mother seemed to Phelps a woman of genius, the inspiration for her own literary career; that she worshipped her cleric-father because he was her sole parent—both led her to create favorite female and male characters accentuating her parents' differences, to the extent that the characters could not have inhabited the same world. The duality had its source in the conflict between female need for achievement and male inability to support that need.

During the period before *Avis,* female protagonists refuse proposals of marriage in both *Hedged In* and *The Silent Partner.* Nixy Trent of *Hedged In* refuses a proposal from the man who had fathered her son because she sees no common ground between people whose experience in life has led them to become "different... forever" (246). Nixy has risen above disadvantaged origins, but her former lover has not. Nixy's friend Christina

Purcell, a secondary female character, suggests the protagonist of Phelps's second period: although she willingly accepts marriage, Phelps makes clear that the man, not the woman, labels the relationship as "love for each other"—a fact that the woman accepts because the man tells her it is so (255– 56). Even though Christina unreservedly accepts marriage, Phelps shows her drawn emotionally to Nixy rather than to the man she will marry. Nixy, not her fiancé, receives Christina's kiss. Finally, on her wedding day she feels as if "buried rather than married" (289). Her close, emotional relationship to Nixy is buried both in a transfer of affection to a husband and in the imminent death of the woman she has loved. The relationship between Nixy and Christina is among the few friendships between female equals in Phelps's novels. Since adequately nurtured by the maternal Margaret Purcell, each had developed a healthy self-confidence; because emotionally secure, neither leaned upon the other.

To avoid a sense of being "buried" as a "silent" partner in a marriage, Perley Kelso of *The Silent Partner* breaks an engagement with an "imperious" fiancé and refuses the proposal of a sympathetic man. She believes that she could not both fulfill the social requirements for being a properly perfect wife and continue to carry out her own self-appointed reform projects for the benefit of millworkers. In allowing Perley to choose public over private useful work, Phelps demonstrates that a marriageable woman might prefer to invest her efforts in a life conducted by herself, rather than become a "silent partner" in a life conducted by a husband. In contrast to *Hedged In*, the secondary female character—Perley's lower-class friend—also refuses a marriage proposal. She would have preferred to marry her suitor; however, she will not because, lacking birth control, she dare not bring children into a sordid mill world from which they cannot escape (chap. 14). A contemporaneous juvenile work, *My Cousin and I* (first published in 1872–1873), also depicts female characters unmarried by choice. In all three instances, women choosing a single life enjoy strong emotional ties with other women. They do not require a marital partner for emotional support.

Several biographical factors may have influenced the fictional refusals of Phelps's first period. Though lacking the security that a living mother would have provided, but experiencing the exuberance of her early advocacy of women's rights and encouraged by her "boon companion's" support, Phelps may have felt able during the early 1870s to imagine the unimaginable—women living together, successfully independent. Bodily invalidism, however, became a counterpoint to the fictional optimism. Before *The Silent Partner* was completed, Phelps became ill and finished the book against her physician's orders. Her health remained poor for some five years, perhaps as a response to disapproval received for having favored the "elevation of her own sex" (*Chapters*, 250). Her father's anti-feminist essays of 1879 and 1881 gave his opposition public visibility. He was her only parent, however, and she worshipped him—a worship that would have made difficult acknowledging the deep hurt his censure caused; so she would experience the hurt, not consciously, but as the ill health of her body. In addition, ill health was a socially acceptable excuse for limiting her public activities. In this way she might control her conflict between innovative thinking about women and her relatively inactive behavior within the woman's movement. On the grounds of ill health, Phelps refused the prolonged and active participation in women's reforms that her views would have warranted. Rather she created innovative women characters.

Though divided against herself, Phelps was sometimes aware of the emotional basis of her sleepless invalidism. A letter to Longfellow stated the connection between experiencing restful sleep and receiving approval from those she respected. Upon another occasion, she wrote to Whittier of "illness" when the context made clear that she experienced emotional stress. In a May, 1877, letter to George Eliot, Phelps explained on the basis of ill health the six-year silence between *The Silent Partner* and *The Story of Avis*. She noted that she was then struggling with a new book, *Avis,* after "many years of enforced silence [from illness]." She continued, "I do not hope much for it now; I am physically too far spent ever to do what it is a bitter comfort to hope I might have done, if the success of 'The Gates Ajar' had not driven a *very* young woman who wanted money, into rapid and unstudious work...."[19]

Four years earlier, in February, 1873, Phelps had written Eliot an evaluation of *Middlemarch* (1872) that suggests a major theme of her own *Avis*—namely, the rejection of "wifehood as a métier" and the exploration of "woman's personal identity," with which Phelps believed "Society had yet to acquaint itself" and was "yet to be revolutionized"; she thought it would "require a *great novel* to proclaim the royal lineage of the Coming Woman to the average mind." But only Eliot could write the great novel: her own would be, "a small one."[20] These two Eliot letters taken together suggest Phelps's aim in *The Story of Avis*. That she should on the one hand take upon herself the challenge that she had urged upon the author of *Middlemarch* (1872), "the novel of the century," suggests the high standards that she set for herself. To be effective in persuading the "average mind" of the "Coming Woman's royal lineage," she must write a "great novel." On the other hand, she declared herself "spent" and unable to do what she "might have done." Just as her father, called to the honor of a chair on the Andover faculty, had become ill before beginning to function in a position for which he felt himself unequal, so the daughter pursued the same pattern. She set her hopes high yet felt herself inadequate. The resulting conflict expressed itself in her disabled body and allowed invalidism to become her rationale for missing the perfection after which, like the rest of her kin, she strove.

The period from 1871 to 1876, at the end of which Phelps wrote *The Story of Avis,* was thus one of mustering her forces to join open battle with the sacred, but suppressing, institutions of marriage and motherhood. If declaring support for women's rights cost her dearly, then how much more would she pay for open criticism of the magnitude she planned? The six-year gap between books was the longest such silence in Phelps's career. As Tillie Olsen notes, "Censorship silences." She continues "Where the gifted ... have never attained full capacity, it is because of circumstances, inner or outer, which oppose the needs of creation."[21]

Although its author was then acknowledged to be "gifted," *Avis* misses being a masterwork, one problem being its stylistic infelicities.[22] But a book so going against cultural expectations could hardly be written easily or smoothly. The style reveals the effort of the writer to overcome inhibitions to her self-expression. Phelps had the courage to say the unsayable—not covertly, as her mother had often done by implication, or as Louisa May Alcott was doing over a pseudonym, but overtly, in the actions and characters of a signed novel.[23]

Beginning the second period of Phelps's interpretation of marriage, *The Story of Avis* depicts a woman who accepts marriage, but thereby experiences disaster. (Such disaster vindicates the marital refusal of earlier protagonists.) The first married protagonist to appear in a Phelps novel, Avis Dobell is also her creator's "favorite heroine" (*Chapters,* 157). Avis derives both from Phelps's mother's life and fiction and from Phelps's own life. In particular, Avis exemplifies Phelps's mother's dying wish for her daughter—namely, that she be trained in the fine arts. That Phelps's mother so skillfully illustrated the stories she wrote for her children suggests that her wish for the daughter was a projection of her own unrealized desire to become an artist, but since training in the fine arts was often unavailable to women, they were diverted to writing—an art they could practice without training.[24]

In Avis, Phelps depicts successful training and explores the meaning for a woman of trying to achieve both domestic and artistic excellence. Phelps shows how, like her mother, Avis as "a wife, a mother, a housekeeper, a hostess...on an academic salary," shoulders a burden if not "deadly," then "deadening" when she starts upon an artistic career.[25] If art is the goal, then marriage is the burden of Avis's life. As in her mother's *The Sunny Side*—at least partially derived from Phelps's grandmother's life—Phelps seeks to expose this burden. Avis becomes Everywoman who aspires to goals that her society has set apart for men and who then finds her striving steps hedged in. The novel thus documents what Phelps considers to be man's distractions to woman's achievement.[26]

These distractions appear primarily in the relationship between Avis and the man she erringly idealizes, Philip Ostrander. Avis first glimpses Philip as a fellow tourist in a Parisian church. She finds his face "remarkable ... like an amber intaglio" (71). Very likely Phelps alludes to "The Amber Gods" (1860) by her friend Harriet Prescott Spofford. In Spofford's story the amber beads of the title cast upon a beloved an inescapable spell, which benefits their owner at the expense of the beloved.[27] Such will be Avis's fate.

Early meetings between Avis and Philip emphasize his egotism and carelessness of others: more concerned to impress, he forgets a hurt bluejay he carries so that it dies. The fate of the bird suggests the fate of Avis's talent—the *rara avis* which, under Philip's thoughtlessness, would die. Although Avis's teacher believes she should paint from her creative imagination and not waste her time with portraits, she paints Philip's portrait. Afterwards he proclaims to Avis that they now love each other. But with the example of her mother's unfulfilled longing for a stage career supplanted by domestic pursuits, Avis determines not to love Philip. In spite of "nineteen centuries of womanhood," Avis chooses a career in art over the profession of marriage (128–30). "In a reckless temper" because of Avis's refusal, Philip enlists in the Civil War (135–36, 164). He reasons that perhaps Avis might mourn him in his death: "war offered the quickest and most incisive road to a glorious solution of inglorious personal difficulties" (164–65).

Unfortunately for Avis, Philip's recklessness wins. Suffering from war wounds, he gains her pity. She senses that she has "taken the first step in a road which led to some undefined but imperative surrender of her nature" (185). Avis's response to Philip's ill health reflects Phelps's life—a succession of men (her brothers, father, and husband) for whom the caring of sickness and the caring of love were inextricably confused. Through Avis's submission, Phelps reveals the price to a woman of the social expectation that she find self-definition in relationships to others and, as a result, ignore her own goals. As a chapter epigraph Phelps quotes from George Eliot's verse drama "Armgart" (1870): "I would with all my soul I knew / The man so rare, that he could make your life / As woman sweet to you, as artist safe" (119).[28] Philip would provide sourness for the woman and danger for the artist.

Before her marriage Avis had nearly completed her master-work, an imposing Sphinx, an image of such importance to the novel that Phelps had originally used as title "The Story of the Sphinx."[29] Avis's subject came to her in a vision. She had first seen a succession of downtrodden souls; then "the room seemed to become full of women"—Cleopatra, Helen, Jeanne d'Arc, Magdalene, Sappho—"a motley company" who "moved on solemnly, and gave way to a silent army of the unknown" (*Avis*, 149). Then

She saw.... the great sphinx, restored. The mutilated face patiently took on the forms and the hues of life: the wide eyes met her own; the dumb lips parted; the solemn brow unbent. The riddle of ages whispered to her. The mystery of womanhood stood before her, and said, "Speak for me." (150)

The Egyptian Great Sphinx of Gizeh, although masculine, was clearly Phelps's model. She drew upon its awesome appearance as well as upon its symbolism of resurrection, royal power, and benevolent guardianship. From the Greek Sphinx of *Oedipus* she took the female sex and riddle of manhood, recast as a riddle of womanhood.

Phelps would pose, but not solve, this riddle. If the Sphinx is Avis's portrait of the dumb riddle of womanhood, then Avis herself is Phelps's Sphinx. Frequently, Avis appears Sphinx-like to those about her; they see her as "a great, dumb, protesting goddess" (115). In the character of Avis, the daughter Phelps made concrete a riddle that she had learned at her mother's knee—how to be both woman and artist.

Gradually Avis forsakes her own need to pursue her art single-mindedly and to answer for womankind the Sphinx's riddle of her ages. She yields to Philip's wish to marry, ignoring her original claim never to have seen a male able to show a woman the "tolerance of individuality" or "enthusiasm of superiority" that lovers think possible (126). Avis finally believes Philip's claim that he will take pride in her genius, encourage her career, and not require her domestic competence.

With marriage, Avis's prospects for a successful career fall while Philip's rise. She has no studio in her husband's house, and domestic difficulties seem a perpetual distraction. Motherhood— "the blindly deifying privilege" of romances—Avis finds "a great deal of trouble" (275, 277). Child care is totally her responsibility, and as its demands render her less aware of other domestic duties, Philip complains "through his teeth" and makes blatantly clear that he does require services from her. Her own career at a standstill, Avis must suddenly try to meet the family's financial needs when Philip is asked to resign his position: his "lack of intellectual constancy" has disappointed the faculty of Harmouth University (317). Under so many burdens, Avis's previously strong physique breaks. Her illness becomes the occasion for Philip to demonstrate his lack of emotional constancy by carrying on a flirtation with Avis's nurse. Philip then leaves to winter in southern France, with the explanation that his lungs require a change of climate.

"Avis was shocked to find her husband's absence a relief" (361). Her creativity had been constrained, not by the facts of marriage or motherhood in themselves, but by the burden they placed upon the woman alone. Removing Philip from the scene removes the husband whose constraining expectations and lack of domestic participation keep Avis from her work. In Philip's absence Avis feels sisterhood with all abandoned, betrayed, and neglected women. In this mood but with "barren brain, and broken heart, and stiffened fingers," Avis hastily completes her painting of the Sphinx to pay debts Philip has left behind him (362, 373).

Following the practices of domestic fiction, Phelps's solution to the demands upon Avis of marriage and motherhood is removing by death the offending characters.[30] Avis's son dies of pneumonia and her husband of consumption. Ironically, the closer Philip comes to death and the heaven of Phelps's Utopian "Gates" series, the more self-awareness he gains. But Phelps was never to depict a marriage satisfactory to a woman. In the world she knew, few men offered their wives the services that they expected to receive. Such a man in fiction would have been a romantic idealization, rather than the realistic "truth" that Phelps sought to present in her art (*Chapters,* 249–66). The social constraints upon Avis reside in the behavior expected of women and men. In paragraphs enthusiastically praised by the *Woman's Journal* Phelps explains her belief that the ideal woman and man of the future would be mutually supportive although not necessarily as marital partners. As Phelps's 1874 ideal of marriage makes clear, she was not against marriage in itself: she was opposed to relationships designed to benefit men to the detriment of women. Women ought to be able to expect the same benefits from marital relationships as men and men ought to provide the same services as women, she believed. Where a man could not treat a woman as an equal, she would be happier without him. Phelps portrayed single womanhood as a desirable and reasonable option—even as late as the 1879 *An Old Maid's Paradise.*[31]

If men as fathers and husbands prevented the full development of a woman of genius, in other roles men might not. To suggest what might have been for Avis had she not succumbed to marriage, Phelps offers two male characters—Avis's former painting master Frederick Maynard, and a neighbor and undeclared suitor Stratford Allen. Frederick treats Avis's talent seriously, sends her to Italy to study, urges her to create from her artistic strength. Stratford, performer of sundry altruistic kindnesses in Harmouth, buys her "Sphinx." That both Frederick and Stratford support Avis suggests to readers that her dream of artistic success was not beyond her reach, and need not have been, except for her succumbing to the pressure to marry a man not strong enough to carry out his promise to support her genius.

Phelps concludes *The Story of Avis* by looking optimistically toward a future in which Avis's one daughter Waitstill (called

Wait) will be adequately prepared to achieve success on her own terms. Named for her Grandmother Ostrander—who had waited throughout old age for a visit from her thoughtlessly absent son—Wait will not repeat the blunders of Avis or her grandmother, Avis determines. To establish in Wait a sense of self-confident freedom, Avis lets her "loose upon the wide Harmouth fields and shore" with "no more restriction than a cricket" so that she becomes "a splendid little animal" (448). Wait is not to be subjected to the "depression of novelty in conduct or opinion" that her foremothers had experienced (449). The program Avis sets for Wait will lead her to develop a self-trust and a clear understanding of her own particular needs, such that she will have the internal strength to remain true to them. As an adult, she need not become embedded in dependent relationships and will be able to refuse involvement with those who would sap her of her own best capacities. With good reason, Avis believes that it will be easier for her daughter "to be alive and be a woman, than it had been for her" (452). Phelps implies that Wait will become a feminine Galahad, finding at last the Grail of fulfilled woman-hood and refusing diversion into consuming domestic entangle-ment (456-57).

But a mere two years later Phelps first alludes to *A Singular Life,* which is to consider a male character totally incompatible with the "Coming Woman," as suggested in Avis's daughter and in descriptions of the ideal woman and man of the future (450-51). Phelps explains that she hopes "to write a book about a man who tried to live like Jesus Christ," this endeavor to be the "singular" characteristic of his life.[32] The position that Phelps allotted to women in the 1895 novel, however, was decidedly subservient compared to that in *Avis* in 1877. The period of the 1880s, that of Phelp's transition to marriage, also marked a transition in her characterization of women and the second stage in her depiction of marriage.

Having demonstrated in *Avis* that a husband could be small support for a talented wife, in *An Old Maid's Paradise* Phelps reverted to her earlier view that women could live happily and effectively with each other, but in an 1886 sequel, Corona too would lean toward marriage. Phelps's new position began to emerge in 1881 with *Friends: A Duet* where she aimed to convey "partial sadness" that her heroine accepts a less-than-ideal marriage in order to obtain companionship.[33] This novel seems to rationalize a compromise in which a woman gives up her attachment to an ideal—her deceased husband—and yields instead to the pressure of a living man. By 1882, in *Doctor Zay*, Phelps hinted at a woman's potentially successful combination of profession and marriage, but, given female education in self-effacement, Dr. Zay with good reason fears that social expectations would undermine her career even though her husband finds professional commitment a desirable aspect of her personality.

In 1883, through Mary of *Beyond the Gates,* and in 1886 through Helen Ritter of "The Madonna of the Tubs" and Corona of *Burglars in Paradise,* Phelps permits the return of a suitor and his successful second chance.[34] Mary in heaven finds herself reunited with a man she knows she might have loved and had not seen for twenty years. Similarly, the story of Helen Ritter's social benevolence among Gloucester fisher-people concludes with her being joined to the man she had loved but with whom she had quarreled (91-93). And Corona, upon the arrival of a former suitor (one with whom she had also quarreled some years before) wonders whether "the most dangerous housebreaker of all" invades her Paradise to claim friendship with her (220).

The ambiguity of marriage for a woman that Phelps showed in fiction written before 1887 changed to exposure of the malaise that a husband could cause a wife. *The Gates Between* appeared in 1887, marking the beginning of the third stage in Phelps's depiction of marriage. Its female character is another Helen, the wife of Phelps's first male protagonist, Dr. Esmerald Thorne. This stage of Phelps's thinking about marriage shows male protagonists who assume emotional support from women in marriage. In Esmerald, Phelps shows a man causing his wife stress although she is a strong, healthy person, in contrast to his patients. Esmerald eventually accuses himself of inadequate concern for wife and child. Phelps legitimizes his perception by giving him the prestigious social position of physician. Where in *Avis* Phelps had used the viewpoint of an omniscient observer, here she uses a first-person narrator, Esmerald himself. The technical difference gives her criticisms the appearance of self-revelation. Rather than antagonizing a male reader by pointing an accusatory finger, Phelps strategically seeks to engage his identification with Thorne's painful self-revelations.

In 1893 Phelps published the first post-marriage book-length fiction not co-authored with her husband—a college story called *Donald Marcy*. True to her observation that the married are "hampered" in what they can say, this was a highly conservative and sentimental view of a young woman's moral guardianship of a young man—and his assumption that he must single-handedly establish a financial base for their marriage. The book offers no challenge to accepted views save a young woman's intellectual acuity—which remains unused.[35]

By the spring of 1894 Phelps had completed one third of *A Singular Life*, a story simmering in her mind since 1879. In fact, the stories appearing between 1880 and 1891 that Phelps collected into *Fourteen to One* (1891) without exception treat issues appearing in this novel—illness, temperance, self-sacrifice, and anticlericalism. In addition, "The Supply at Saint Agatha's"—appearing in *Century* (1894) and later reissued as a gift book (1896)—had as its hero a latter-day Christ. In a letter to her publisher, Henry Oscar Houghton, she described the novel as a "religious story... laid in a theological town but chiefly in a fishing place. The hero is a man who 'tries to live like Christ'—this bringing upon himself all sorts of apparent defeat...." Phelps appeared to believe that *A Singular Life* (serialized in the *Atlantic Monthly*) presents a totally regenerate male character in Emanuel Bayard, since he was her favorite among her male characters as was Avis among her female (*Chapters*, 157, 273). Audiences agreed with her: the book immediately drew a good sale and had reached a total of 54,000 copies within four years. More in accord with mainstream culture than *Avis*, it was also stylistically more controlled.[36]

But Phelps's choice of favorites reveals her opposing expectations for women and men, an opposition which she seemed unable to resolve. *The Story of Avis* had depended upon her knowledge of women living with professional men—particularly such a woman as her mother. *A Singular Life* depended upon her knowledge of those professional men—her grandfathers, father, and brothers. But Phelps herself had been a temperance worker in Gloucester during the summers from 1875 to 1879, as she described in her autobiography. She recasts the experiences in which she, a woman, acted the role of pastor to a flock, as the experience of a man: particularly feminine aspects of her experience she presents in Emanuel's wife Helen. Phelps's savior of needy people was no longer a Winifred Forceythe, a Margaret Purcell, or a Perley Kelso, but rather an Emanuel Bayard. In him Phelps created a man who tries to live like Christ as a pastor to his flock—and who like Christ meets martyrdom. Of particular interest in this novel is the destiny of the women surrounding a Christ-like man.

Phelps had used Gloucester fishing-folk in two previous tales that she combines in the Job Slip family of this novel. In both versions—each collected in *Fourteen to One*—she recognized the women's hard lot, which she barely acknowledges in the 1895 novel. The first version was "The Madonna of the Tubs," featuring laundress Ellen Jane Salt, who provides her fisherman-husband with "all the little feminine arts that make men cheerful at the cost of women's nerve and courage" (54). A second version of the Slip family appeared in 1887 as "Jack," where Phelps makes the temperance problem central, as in *A Singular Life*.[37] She explains the deprivations leading Jack to alcohol. For a while Mother Mary, an effective woman preacher, helps Jack; analogous to Helen Ritter in "Madonna of the Tubs," she is an autobiographical prototype for Emanuel. Later, in drunken anger and jealousy, Jack blindly strikes and kills his wife. Although a deficient environment ruins him, a trusting woman suffers even more than he. Not a Mother Mary but Emanuel Bayard would aid Job Slip, the fictional descendent of Jack. Although Emanuel would observe that he "never knew what a woman could suffer" until he met Job's wife, he would devote his attention to men's needs and remain oblivious of the cost to women of his Christ-like life (168).

The need most prominent in Emanuel's eyes is the control of liquor. As early as 1881 Phelps had suggested through the words of Reliance Strong that one day someone would "do for these poor slaves [to drink] what Harriet Stowe did for the black ones" (*Friends,* 126). In an 1887 letter Phelps noted that "more than half of the success of 'Jack' is owing to its great moral story; as with 'Uncle Tom' on the larger plan."[38] Emanuel is her fictional savior of the drink-ridden poor. He will act on two fronts—privately to save families from the drunken rages of bread-winners, as represented by Job Slip, and publicly to control the liquor business, as represented by Ben Trawl. Emanuel's dual involvement reveals not only the damage wrought by liquor in beaten wives and children, but also the benefits to grog shop owners, whose financial interest "the churches would back" (248). Through his home mission, called "The Love of Christ" or "Christlove," Emanuel reforms men away from the grog shops so successfully that business decreases. This success in saving others' lives now endangers his own. He achieves "a deadlock between the rum interest and the decent citizens" (326). Although Emanuel forfeits his life to a stone hurled by Ben Trawl, Job Slip sturdily maintains that "He's lingerin' in us poor devils he's spent three years makin' men of..." (422).

In addition to being a pro-temperance novel, *A Singular Life* is anticlerical. Emanuel's ordination council is concerned less with social conscience than with theology (chap. 5). While a theo-logue, he was not "taught how to save drunken men" (145); his professor "had been so occupied with the misery of the next world that he had never investigated the hell of this one" (385). Phelps implies that practice, not doctrine, should have been the subject of study. Actively living a Christian "social gospel" is what makes Emanuel Bayard's life "singular" (152, 389). Phelps draws obvious parallels between the life of Jesus and that of Emanuel—birth in Bethlehem of parents named Joseph and Mary, rejection by the established church, successful ministry among the powerless, and death at the hands of established power. The total effacement of death in a complete sacrifice of self is the wage of a truly Christian life, for which the church offers no shelter.

The women surrounding Emanuel Bayard reveal, however, the price they pay for his Christ-like martyrdom, an issue not recognized as such by Phelps, who presents Emanuel favorably. She includes three women—a street girl Lena, his unmarried nurse and housekeeper Jane, and his future wife Helen. The character Lena is less dependent upon Emanuel than other women surrounding him, but Phelps treats her less generously than she had Nixy, the unmarried mother of *Hedged In.* On the one hand, Emanuel refuses to recognize the social distance typically maintained between a minister and a street girl by treating Lena (her name undoubtedly derived from "Magdalena")[39] as equally worthy of his concern as drunken fishermen. Nonetheless he believes that she must not make herself respectable by working as a domestic—presumably because she might thus contaminate "pure" women—but must rather work in a gunpowder factory— potentially dangerous work, by implication appropriate for dispensable people. Yet, despite his limited concern, she risks her life to see that justice is brought to his murderer. Phelps sees nothing unsatisfactory in Emanuel's treatment of Lena.

She is more sympathetic to the suffering of Jane and her mother, Mrs. Granite, who run the boarding house where Emanuel lodges. He remains oblivious to the energies they expend upon him. Without Jane's affectionate care, he would have lacked both time and energy to pursue his reforms: "suffering and helpless, he...needed her. Busy and well, he thought of her no more" (196). At the end, Jane enjoys the "precious chance" of ministering to Emanuel's needs for his last eight days (417). For her self-effacing devotion Jane receives from him only a copy of Coleridge's "Kubla Khan," but she gives him "self-forgetful service" for the duration of his boarding (196, 417). Phelps observes that "the best of men may work his share of heart-break, and the better he is the less he will suspect it" (197). That she could have labeled Emanuel "best" when he blindly causes such "heart-break" indicates her own "hampered" view. Married,

Phelps could not openly censure the behavior she had previously decried; she appears resigned to shortcomings she had earlier believed remediable.

The character most revealing of Emanuel's attitudes toward women is his future wife, Helen, the dutiful but irreverent daughter of Professor Carruth. She appears to be a fictional descendent of Helen Ritter ("Madonna of the Tubs") and Helen Thorne (*Gates Between*). Like the first Helen, she acts the benefactress to a fishing family—Job, Mari, and Joey Slip—and in so doing impresses Emanuel with her womanly, though unorthodox, solutions to his parishioners' problems. Like the second Helen, she devotes herself to a man's career and shows no concern for her own needs. Emanuel dreams of Helen—"a woman capable of understanding the highest and serving it, capacious for tenderness and yielding to it, a woman warm, human, sweet, and as true as one's belief in her"—and hopes that she will "pour the precious current of her love into [his] long life's work" (239-40). If such should happen, Emanuel believes he "would be a god! He would climb the inaccessible. He would achieve the undreamed and the unknown" (240). Emanuel in his over-idealization of self accepts without question Helen's effacement of self. Although he claims that he will take responsibility for Helen, in fact his expectation that her worshipful love will deify him places responsiblity for his godliness upon her (342). The traditional Victorian marital quid pro quo entails masculine economic for feminine moral protection, even when the husband is a clergyman.

Once Emanuel is financially able to marry Helen, he exhibits toward her an "imperious" stance: he expects her to obey his wishes because he loves her. Yet in contrast to artist Avis Dobell, reformer Reliance Strong, and physician Zaidee Atalanta Lloyd, Helen is an eager spouse, glad to help her husband's people. When a plot against Emanuel's life becomes known, Helen willingly advances the date of their marriage.

Their honeymoon behind them, the Bayards return for the dedication of a new chapel. When Emanuel, with Helen at his side, descends the chapel steps, "hate struck and he fell transfigured" (409). Phelps, having planned such Christian martyrdom for Emanuel, again as in *Friends: A Duet* and *Doctor Zay*, would not show her readers happy marriage. The last hours of Emanuel's life show this man of God surrounded by three women devoted to his welfare, existing not for themselves but for their parts in his life. Phelps sets up a hierarchy of awareness whereby Emanuel is as oblivious of their deep concern for him as are orthodox theologians uncomprehending of his concern for the personal lives of his flock (197).

Although this favorite male character practices religious heresy, thereby indicating Phelps's criticism of a male clergy, his behavior toward women is traditional. Phelps could not relinquish her expectation of godliness in men: "godliness" seems to have meant "authority," the basis for commanding others. This worship of the male as a God-like superbeing kept a worshipper from realizing her own potential. God's being perceived as male, his deputies traditionally being so, legitimized maleness in a way that femaleness could never be. Likewise, the excessively high expectations that such affinity with godhead placed upon men could only have created comparably excessive anxiety. In fact, woman's worship rather than man's self-discipline was confidently expected to keep a man "manly" (*Avis,* 196; *Life,* 240). But the limitations of the life she called "singular" Phelps was unable to explore. Nevertheless, *A Singular Life* demonstrates how Christian belief reinforcd marital hierarchy.

In the same year that *A Singular Life* was published, Elizabeth Cady Stanton brought out Part I of *The Woman's Bible*.[40] Neither Phelps nor women who read her novel are likely to have read Stanton's *Bible*. The novel is, nonetheless, a realistic representation of the implications for women of this *Bible*. Stanton had collected all passages from Old and New Testaments having to do with women. Then she had a committee write commentaries demonstrating how these passages, basic to Christian theology, consistently demeaned women. Phelps's novel shows in fiction what the ideal of a Christian woman led to. Appropriately, Phelps develops Helen Carruth only vaguely: the "singular life" is Emanuel's. Helen's very subordination, however, supports the view Phelps had advanced in Avis Dobell and Helen Thorne—

that marriage to professional men benefited not women, as typically claimed, but men. Phelps's *Singular Life* thus vindicated Stanton's *Woman's Bible*.

Fictional Favorites: Her Ambivalence

The contrast between Phelps's explicit criticism of marriage in *Avis* and her acknowledgment of the constraints Helen would have experienced in a marriage to Emanuel is revealing of changed attitudes. Earlier in her career Phelps struggled to overcome personal stress and to gather psychological strength to expose in *Avis* the plight of women. Hostile response to so honest a portrayal as *Avis* perhaps suggests that she had broken a taboo upon a woman's openly criticizing the institution of marriage. As a result, we can assume that such hostility kept her from again portraying a marriage through a woman's eyes (save over a pseudonym in 1902). Next, as she herself moved toward marriage, she tried criticizing the role assigned women in marriage by depicting a male character, Esmerald Thorne. But apparently no critique of marriage was possible after her 1888 marriage. In addition, her father's 1890 death may have rendered her, out of deference to his passing from her life, no longer able to criticize openly the ramifications for women of the values that he had reverenced during his life—namely, those of the clerical life. As his descendent, she became a standard-bearer responsible for maintaining his values. *A Singular Life* was preceded by *Austin Phelps: A Memoir* (1891) and followed by *The Story of Jesus Christ: An Interpretation* (1897). In each she sought to present in the most favorable light possible the Christian life as lived by a man. Her view of "Jesus the Friend," however, was a gender-free interpretation of deity, in contrast to her father's belief in "God the Father."

In addition to the effect of adult experience upon Phelps's reduced attention to women's problems, her father's death may have activated childhood resentment over her mother's death. In spite of Phelps's intended favorable view of Emanuel's "singular life," as in *Avis*, the husband must die: here that death bears a larger symbolic weight. If Bayard is in any way a memorial to her father (as I believe he is), that death is of the father as well as of the husband. If the worship of women displayed by husbands and sons paralleled that of men by wives or daughters, then Phelps's worship of her father must also have been grounded in awe, fear, and even resentment. As a mother to a son, he was to her the powerful, opposite-sexed parent, to whose identity (as professor of theology) she had no access. To the awe and fear so established must, in Phelps's case, be added a severely repressed resentment: upon her father's "feudal views" she partially blamed the death of her mother (*Chapters*, 12, 15; *A. Phelps*, 87-89). If Phelps could never put behind her the sense of loss that she felt from being only eight years old when her mother died, then she must also have harbored, even though largely unacknowledged, a resentment toward the man she imagined responsible for this loss. Even so remote an expression of parental resentment as the death of Emanuel she could not attempt until after her father died.

A third factor that may account for Phelps's emphasis at this time upon men's lives and avoidance of women's problems is the historical trend of women toward establishing emotional ties less with each other and more with men.[41] Phelps's characterizations show such a pattern. Thus we find that Nixy Trent and Christina Purcell openly embrace; Perley Kelso and Sip Garth join to ameliorate millworkers' lives; Avis enjoys a lifelong friend in Coy Bishop; Reliance Strong shares for a short time the company of a fellow reformer, Myrtle Snowe; Dr. Zay refuses female companionship altogether; and Lena, Jane Granite, and Helen Carruth contend to offer service to one man. Phelps's favorite woman and her favorite man are poorly matched: for her art, Avis needed no spouse; for his ministry, Emanuel required a wife. Choosing as favorites characters who could not have lived in the same world suggests that Phelps had changed the construction of her world (*Chapters*, 157, 273). Rather than criticizing a marital condition unfavorable to women, as she had in *Avis*, Phelps reveals a world gone awry, which only the miracle of a vulnerable male Christ might be able to save. Her view was far more pessimistic than in her pre-marriage novels. Job Slip gives up rum, but of the women who surround Emanual we have little suggestion of their benefit or future. Phelps shows no awareness of what her characterizations reveal of women's fate. Following the historical trend to become emotionally attached to imperious men rather than to supportive women, she showed her women to be doomed to self-effacement. She never recognized, let alone resolved, the contradiction implicit in choosing as favorites Avis and Emanuel.

From her marriage in 1888 to about 1900 Phelps's views about women underwent significant change. No longer did her fictional women "dream and dare"; rather they would "yield" and "serve" a man's work instead of their own. And, instead of women, men were now the protagonists. From 1870 to 1882 Phelps had shown women faring better in an environment peopled by women than in one headed by men. In her fiction support for men's lives is institutionalized in their marriages or in the subordinate relationship to them of female relatives or servants; support for women's lives receives no institutionalization, but rather must come from informal networks, always subject to interference from men.

Besides being more conservative in her fiction, Phelps was less active in supporting women's rights. Although she was listed as an "occasional contributor" to the *Woman's Journal* from 1884 until after 1895, and was made an honorary member of the Andover Woman Suffrage League in May, 1887, she seems to have retired from active involvement in the women's movement after her marriage. In 1889 she established a "Fisherman's Reading Room." In 1890 an article on women's dress appeared, a sentimental and stereotypic view when contrasted with her articles of the 1870s.[42]

By 1896 the fire had burned out of her pen. Scarcely a decade before the publication of her autobiography, one writer in the *Woman's Journal* believed that Phelps, not Howells, was the "greatest novelist" in America because, where Howells "jostles" nobody and puts women and men into separate worlds, Phelps "shakes up and wakes up" and puts both sexes into one world. "Our Queen Elizabeth of literature is of to-morrow and all the rest of time," the writer, who called herself "Sojourner," concluded.[43] By 1900, however, Phelps's best work was completed: she had tried verses and stories for adults and children, as well as essays and novels. At age 56, she would never again receive the acclaim that her "Gates" and feminist novels had brought before her marriage. Her own need to marry, coupled with the increasing conservatism of the women's movement after the 1890s, prevented her from ever resolving the ambivalence revealed in her choosing as favorites characters who could never have inhabited the same world—namely, a woman for whom marriage was disastrous and a man for whom marriage was essential.

Chapter Five
Final Years

The final seven of twenty-five novels by Elizabeth Stuart Phelps are the work of a tired woman and lack the energetic conviction of her fiction from the 1870s and 1880s. She offers no innovative solutions to women's need for fulfillment or equality in relationships with men. Instead, from 1901 to 1908 she reworked previous material. From having concentrated upon male figures during the 1890s, she returns to her emphasis upon women—but her women have become spineless, dependent for their well-being upon the presence of sympathetic servants or men. Contrary to her earlier fiction, all upper-middle-class women accept marriage; only one housekeeper retains emotional independence. Marriages in process are no happier than in the earlier fiction, but the happy ending required by editors (namely, that a marriage occur or survive) always appears.[1] No matter what her previous problems, the newly engaged woman or the wife of a reformed husband might anticipate a happy marriage, but only after the novel's end. Phelps maintains her earlier view that marital happiness for women resides in some other life than the present. Since her experience did not show her how marriage could be fulfilling to a woman, her accommodation to "happy endings" was as grudging as she could manage without sacrificing her need to be published.

Her Last Novels

Phelps's own diminished confidence as a woman appears in the prevalence of female characters dependent upon males. These characterizations confirm the historical trend, which began in the 1880s, of women viewing with increasing distaste emotional ties between women. Even women from the so-called upper-middle-class "feminist" group turned away from "intense emotional, sensual commitment between women to have a more ambivalent, less committed form of relationship."[2]

Two novels from this period—*The Successors of Mary the First* and *Avery*—show an invalid wife dependent upon the help of a capable maid or a reformed husband. The earlier novel, *The Successors of Mary the First* (1901)—serialized in the *Ladies' Home Journal*—is cast in the humorous style of her "Paradise" tales, but here "Home" replaces "Paradise."[3] A panorama of women serve the Hollis household from the first Mary, who lives in for thirteen years, to her thirteen successors, who file through in one year. Once again Phelps acknowledges the debt women owe to the maids who keep their households running smoothly. Perley Peace Hollis, energetic clubwoman in suburban Sweet Home, maintains her health only while she has competent household help. Her husband George, principal of the local high school, has the "dreamy eyes" of a man whose wife shelters him from "domestic fret" and makes his home a "well of rest" (11); he is incapable of comprehending that, ill, Perley can no longer provide for him. Perley's resilient daughter, thirteen-year-old Hazel, assumes household responsibility during her mother's illness. Her newspaper advertisement for a maid, in which she offers a room with a fire, results in an outpouring of applications—"far more than [authorship's] usual returns," Phelps quips (176). But those applications accurately reflect the desperation of untrained women for whom domestic service is the only available work. The thirteenth applicant, Kathia Maiden, remains in the Hollis household because of mutual satisfaction. Unlike previous maids, Kathia will not reside in a fireless attic room, but instead uses Perley's former sewing room, refurnished according to her own taste—considerations Phelps advocates to her readers.

Not only does Kathia's miraculous management restore Perley's health and marriage, but she also becomes the object of Hazel's love. Contrary to historical trend, Phelps again shows women's emotional attachments for each other—Perley's for Mary I, Hazel's for Kathia—as resolutions of life's problems or as sources of pleasure. In an introductory "Note," she observes, "For so sacred and so subtle is the power of a human home, that those who have ever formed one family can never be or become to one another like strangers without the gates" (iv). The language of *Mary The First* ties it both to the Utopian "Gates" and the humorous "Paradises." But the diction of the "Paradise" tales, previously associated with a woman's independence, Phelps here attaches to a competent servant's creation of domestic bliss. Kathia, "used to taking her happiness by proxy," resigns herself to a "sacrificial" demeanor and, homeless, carries her "Kingdom of Home" within her (267). After 1900 Phelps replaced the Utopia of an independent Paradise with dependence upon "capable, honorable, and lovable women who ... give ... happiness in giving ... service" at Home (iv). In addition, with her health increasingly failing and life's end approaching, Home became a more attractive symbol of Utopia than the heavenly afterlife of her "Gates" series.[4] Phelps continued to create in her fiction what lay beyond her reach in life. She returned to an earlier solution: *The Successors of Mary the First* offers female-female support as the underlying answer to women's needs, since a woman cannot rely upon understanding from a husband.

Her next work, the novelette *Avery* (1902), reverses the solution: not a capable maid but a reformed husband smooths a woman's life. Originally serialized in *Harper's New Monthly* as "His Wife," *Avery* develops the tragic side of a theme in the comic *Mary the First*, namely, a husband's inability to accept his wife's illness.[5] In lawyer Marshall Avery, Phelps depicts an inconsiderate and self-serving man, who expects unflagging perfection in his wife Jean, her heart condition notwithstanding. For instance, dissatisfied with Jean's effort to relieve his toothache, he rushes to his dentist, Armstrong, unobservantly leaving her with a heart attack in progress. While anesthetized, Marshall experiences a nightmare in which his neglect causes Jean's death: comprehension dawns that his presumptuous stance of superiority toward her limits his perception to what fits his own needs. Consciousness regained, elated that "that brute ... never did it," Marshall rushes home to find that Jean in fact does appear to be dead (101). Miraculously, Jean's physician Esmerald Thorne revives her while a contrite Marshall questions such interference with the peace and sanctity that apparent death confers upon the once-suffering. However undeservedly, Marshall receives a second chance. Complimented as a miracle worker, Esmerald requires of Marshall that he now work the greater "miracle of love" (11, 121).

At least two explanations for the conclusion of Marshall's unearned reward are possible. One is that the "miracles" of *Mary the First* and *Avery*, as well as the heavens of the 1883 and 1887 "Gates" books, are supra-real, suggesting the impossibility of real-life solutions: "belief in miracles can preserve vestiges of humanity when the essentials of human life are completely suppressed."[6] Such reliance upon the supra- or supernatural thus expresses despair. A second explanation for the discontinuous conclusion lies in the requirement of a happy ending. Phelps complies, but sets her own terms by twice reducing Marshall to despair. A woman married to a man who so marshalled her life could not be well, Phelps implies, for typically such ill health suggests female malaise and deprivation. Phelps conceals as a dream the insensitivity that causes sick lives. (In *The Confessions of a Wife*, the novel that followed *Avery*, Phelps would conceal her own identity by using a pseudonym and present the insensitivity as reality.)

More necessary to Jean than Marshall is the physician, Esmerald Thorne. In *The Gates Between* Phelps subjects Esmerald, in his role as husband, to a painful awakening in a feminized heaven where he must expiate his previous lack of concern for his wife. In *Avery* Esmerald, in his role as life-saving physician, revives Jean, a woman suffering from a "marked weakness of the heart"—a condition in Phelps's characters suggesting inadequate love (9). In effecting such recovery, an impersonal male specialist replaces the strong, motherly female neighbor or relative, who in Phelps's earlier work helped her less able sisters. A contrast between man as spouse and man as friend to woman occurs regularly in Phelps's novels. Typically her women prefer—or learn that they should have preferred—the friend.

The Confessions of a Wife (1902) is her first full-length novel since *Avis* to treat a woman's marital woe. To avoid again being subject to the hostility *Avis* had aroused, Phelps used the pseudonym "Mary Adams." "Mary" was the Christian name her mother had given her, "Adams" her paternal grandmother's family name. But in spite of her efforts at anonymity, the *Woman's Journal* alleged that she had written the *Century* serialization.[7]

In addition, the pseudonym may have been camouflage for Phelps's knowledgeable discussion of drug addiction and its cure. In *Chapters from a Life* Phelps urges that her readers "scorn the habit of using anodynes" if they hope to recover and if they value their reason: as if to protect an intimate, she mysteriously intones, "This revelation is sealed with seven seals." Advertisements in the *Woman's Journal* in the years around 1900 suggest that drug addiction was a problem of sufficient magnitude to warrant publicizing a painless cure for morphine, opium, and cocaine habits. With no more than the sealed warning of *Chapters* as evidence, we cannot know whether Phelps's knowledge came from her own experience or that of someone whose identity she wished to protect, but clearly she understood narcotics.[8]

Confessions is strikingly like *Avis* though less disciplined—as if its author experienced even more internal conflict in writing it and was thus less able to control her material. Phelps's thirteen-year marriage apparently gave her no cause to diminish her case against the institution. The story relates the courtship, marriage, and motherhood of Marna Trent; the drug addiction and departure of her husband Dana Herwin; and their mutual rescue by Marna's physician and former suitor Robert Hazelton. Phelps repeats four themes prominent in *Avis*: the well-concealed bondage that marriage exacts of a woman, the confinement of a woman who has become a mother, the relief that artistic self-expression gives her, and the support that a male friend can render.

Like Philip in *Avis*, Dana Herwin wins Marna's love against her will. Like Avis, Marna wishes she could "unlove" Dana and blames his persistence even though she has made clear her preference for a writing career. Once married, Marna feels herself increasingly surrounded by illusions and repressed truths: marriage inflicts a solitary, silent bondage upon a woman as well as blame for her husband's anger or failure in romance.

The birth of a daughter increasingly restricts Marna's life. Similar to Philip in *Avis*, Dana becomes infatuated with a too available woman, and consequently less aware of Marna's need. Marna devotes herself to her daughter Marion, but Dana criticizes Marna for narrowing herself to a domestic horizon, a narrowness he has aggravated by ignoring her. Ill with grippe, he insists upon laudanum; several months later he departs for a foreign assignment without consulting her.

Marna's breaking heart, like Jean Avery's heart disease, defies her control, and she lapses into a delirium during which she perceives manhood and womanhood at "civil war." Ever loyal Robert Hazelton rescues Marna from sickness, as he had earlier her daughter Marion. She then relieves her mind by writing a "Book of the Heart" to warn women of their bondage to men in marriage and to show that the safer and saner relationship is a friendship such as Robert provides. From *Avis* to *Confessions* Phelps enlarges the role of supportive man and eliminates that of a female friend. Thus she reduces the female world while she enlarges the male world and also makes it more hospitable—if a woman declines to marry.

Like Esmerald in *Avery*, however, Robert's final expression of selfless concern is coaching Dana and Marna through Dana's drug withdrawal and thereby saving their marriage. But in view of all that precedes, the saved marriage merely suits the required happy ending. Dana's self-indulgent addiction and subsequent departure hardly deserve reward. Since Marna must bear unequally (even if willingly) the burden for Dana's recovered well-being, she decides that he must bear the knowledge of all her thoughts; therefore she gives him her "Book of the Heart of the Wife." Dana agrees that Robert is the best man he has ever known and reaffirms his love for Marna. But Marna, in a fleeting glance from Robert, reads from the "book" of his heart that he loves her still.

Although Phelps suggests that a married woman's restriction to a domestic world is her husband's fault, she undercuts her point by making drug addiction account for Dana's behavior. The drug addiction may have been a strategy to account for views so dissident; thus, the more misused Marna is, the greater can be her disillusion. On the other hand, the drug addiction may suggest excessive male self-addiction: Dana initially takes an opiate from self-concern. Where in *Doctor Zay* a man's recovery depends upon an independent woman, in *Confessions* Dana's recovery depends upon Marna, backed by her friend Robert. The woman able to depend upon her own strength disappears from Phelps's work. The problem becomes whether a wife must submit to such masculine assumptions as Dana exhibits or whether she may rely upon the concerned support of a friendly Robert.

The next two novels—*Trixy* and *The Man in the Case*—demonstrate Phelps's tendency after 1900 to give the nurturing male friend an increasingly close and permanent relationship to a woman. Both conclude with the engagement or marriage of a woman to the man who has been understanding of her throughout. In a reversal of the young woman who must prove herself worthy of the fairy-tale prince, these men each must earn the princess.

Trixy (1904), the only novel of this period not first serialized, continues the method of the previous two novels in contrasting two male characters, a "kind" versus an "imperious" man. The issue of vivisection provides the context within which Phelps reveals the men's characters. The plot concerns the recovery of "stolen property"—two pet dogs—from the research laboratory of a medical school: the circumstance recalls an *Atlantic* story, "Loveliness" (1899), which appeared as a small gift book. Both lawyer Philip Surbridge and medical researcher Olin Steele are attracted to the heroine, Miriam Lauriat, a motherless philanthropist, whose companion until its disappearance has been her spaniel Caro.[9]

Like Marna Trent, Miriam writes, but under a pen name for fear of being identified; like Avis, she paints, but only in pastels for her own pleasure. Like Reliance Strong, she engages in charitable activities to escape loneliness and be useful to others. In addition, like Perley Kelso, she is a tenement owner, maintaining her properties in sanitary condition and personally overseeing her tenants. Of particular concern to her is a crippled protégé, Dan Badger, whose performing poodle, Trixy—his source of

livelihood—has disappeared. Both dogs—Trixy and Caro—
eventually reappear, caged in the vivisection laboratory of Galen
Medical School, where Olin Steele conducts his research.

At first Olin finds experimentation upon animals distasteful,
but gradually he succumbs to pressure to pursue research. In time
he finds in Miriam a woman able to keep pace with him as no
other woman had. To his proposal, Miriam responds that she
wants not a husband but a friend. Because Olin believes the world
divided into male rulers and female subjects, he fails to understand her view. By contrast, Philip, Miriam's lawyer, shares in the
management of her economic affairs and in her philanthropic
endeavors. His concerns for Miriam free her, whereas Olin's
determination to win her, as if the spoils of a victory in battle,
make her feel "caged"—an image that connects the woman to the
pets used for experimentation.

Phelps's anti-vivisection concern appears to be an indirect
expression of her feminist interests. Her 1869 support for the
elevation of her sex receded into the less direct temperance work
of the late 1870s. At that stage she concerned herself with
changing men's behavior in order to improve women's lives. By
the mid-1890s, she had moved back one more step to the anti-
vivisection issue. Here the link to feminism was symbolic. In a
later novel (*Though Life Us Do Part*, 1908) Phelps would
observe regarding the risks for a woman in marrying, "A man
may vivisect a women nerve by nerve, anguish by anguish;
nobody knows it. She never cries out" (56), and later in the same
novel she would observe that the world is full of women enduring
the lives that men inflict (165). The heroine of the novel is
named Cara, a similarity not to be overlooked to the dog named
Caro. Phelps suggests that women were treated by men as pets,
vivisected as experimental subjects.

In the three years immediately preceding the publication of
Trixy, Phelps with her husband's agreement had delivered three
addresses on anti-vivisection to the Massachusetts State Legislature. What particularly disturbed her was "the infliction of avoid-
able torture by the powerful upon the weak, by the human
intellect and the human hand upon the helpless body and the

dumb soul," terminology that could refer to men's treatment of women as well as vivisectionists' of dogs.[10] (In *Avis* she had also emphasized through the Sphinx the dumbness of weak and powerless women.) Revealingly, only on this issue could she muster the physical strength to make public speeches; never could she do so on direct behalf of women's rights. Perhaps the significant factor was the support of an approving male colleague, her husband; she dedicated *Trixy* to Ward and calls him her "collaborator" on the novel ("Dedication").

As in *A Singular Life*, however, Phelps recast her own experience as that of a man: Philip argues the cause of anti-vivisection while Miriam waits patiently at home. Miriam shows no reservations about marrying and is the only heroine about whose partner Phelps reveals no undesirable traits. Since she dedicated the novel to her husband, Phelps may have intended it to honor him in the character of Philip Surbridge. Or perhaps since Phelps called him her "collaborator," Ward's influence is evident in the active character's being male, a characteristic of *The Burglar Who Moved Paradise*, Ward's alleged sequel to her *Burglars in Paradise*.

In contrast to *Trixy*, Phelps initially presents with qualification the male friend in *The Man in the Case* (1906). A mystery serialized in the *Ladies' Home Journal*, the tale in spite of its title concerns the problems of a woman, Joan Dare.[11] Her behavior is controlled by the presence in her home of a man whose identity she cannot reveal to her friends and neighbors. Her "case" leads neighbors to speculate wildly about the nature of her relationship to the man and finally to condemn her for what they cannot understand. Small-town slander at its worst ostracizes her. Her pastor's sermon to his flock at the novel's close draws a parallel between Joan Dare and Jeanne d'Arc: like her predecessor, Joan is a successful female warrior. The Reverend Eliakim Cotton chastises the community because they have murdered Joan's character whereas the brother whom she had protected had only taken a life.

Darum S. Dare, the brother, had been the unintentional murderer of a man with whom he had drunkenly quarreled. Joan cares

for him, now ill with consumption. Darum seems to lack awareness of the price his presence exacts from his sister, but at the
time of his death he writes a letter expressing his gratitude for
her care, his chagrin at his cost to her, and his anger at the
supposed Christian community's lack of trust in her. As with
Hedged In, a woman's ostracism occurs as a result of one man's
behavior. Joan's maid, Mary Caroline, notes that menfolks are "a
passel of sp'ild boys" who should not be loose in the same world
where women could "sp'ile 'em," that this is unfair to both
parties. Mary Caroline, a literary descendent of the comically
feminist Puelvir from the "Paradise" books, provides the support
that keeps Joan's life bearable. But, surprisingly, given her conviction that men are to blame for women's sorrows, Mary Caroline marries the "furnace man"—a striking contrast to Puelvir,
who had evaded with clever determination the attentions of the
"raspberry man."

Like her maid, Joan also marries her persistent suitor, architect
Douglas Ray. At the outset Douglas enters the Dare home with
"masterful ease," makes Joan feel both "captured in a prison cell"
and suffocated as she agrees to an engagement (16, 23). Douglas
accepts Joan's feelings as the mystery of womanhood, but small
mystery resides in these phenomena when placed in the context
of Phelps's presentation of marriage as subordination and loss of
independence for women. Joan, as her father's sole known dependent, inherits his social leadership of the community as well as
her own economic independence. Married, she would lose the
freedom to enjoy that position and would feel the constraint of
subordination to another. But Phelps allows Douglas the vision
to accept Joan's terms. By never commanding her, Douglas, like
Philip Surbridge, earns her. Nevertheless, on her wedding day
Joan's "face looked . . . through the illusion with which the custom
of generations has blurred the eyes of a bride" (246). Typically,
Phelps allows us to follow the couple no further.

The last two novels—*Walled In* and *Though Life Us Do
Part*—depict the uncertain outcome of marriage. Serialized in
Harper's Bazar, Walled In: A Novel (1907) continues to examine
men's thoughtlessness toward women as well as women's caring

for disabled men.[12] The status of Phelps's caring woman, however, has declined since the 1882 *Doctor Zay*, where the woman was a competent physician pursuing an active practice. In *Man in the Case* the woman was a sister with no particular training at all. In this novel, since the wife Teasie Ferris proves unwilling, the caring woman is her sister Honor Tryde, a graduate nurse. Though Honor would prefer being a physician, her stepfather thought nursing more appropriate. Phelps can no longer show a Dr. Zay in full possession of herself and her chosen career.

With *Walled In* Phelps takes the male rather than the female viewpoint. In fact, the main character, Myrton Ferris, a professor of Routledge College, incorporates characteristics of her father, Austin Phelps. If in Emanuel Bayard, Phelps had depicted what her father idealized, in Myrton Ferris she portrays what he actually became—a disabled man requiring a nurse's care for his last years.

Myrton, permanently crippled from an accident in his steam carriage—an invention whose dangers were far more evident to Phelps than its advantages—is "walled in." Confined to his bed, Myrton finds life particularly difficult because his wife Teasie fails to spare her husband the practical aspects of running a household and cannot cope with sickness. Myrton finds his dog's companionship more reliable than people's—a common theme in Phelps's last fiction.

But Myrton could blame himself for his mistake in marrying Teasie, since he had thoughtlessly persisted until she yielded to his proposal. Teasie, Myrton's second wife and mother of his son Trip, expresses her duty as a professor's wife in a simultaneously maternal and coquettish attitude toward students. But the dilemma of an attractive woman caught in an incompatible marriage was beyond Phelps's capacity to solve. Teasie and a student drown after their canoe capsizes. A gender reversal of Marshall Avery in her insensitivity to her spouse, Teasie must die where he was allowed to reform.

In contrast to Teasie, Honor sacrifices herself for Myrton as any good woman does, Phelps implies. Like Waldo Yorke in *Doctor Zay*, Myrton loves the woman who cares for him. Honor accepts his proposal because she loves him and believes she can help him even though she must sacrifice her career as a surgical nurse. In fact, the female behavior approved in the book—Honor's willing self-sacrifice for Myrton—guarantees the perpetuation of female subordination to male desire. Such willingness to be used begs for a user.

Like other male characters in Phelps's novels, Myrton's disability qualifies him for the care of a good woman. Perhaps initially learned from the example of a blinded Romney Leigh in Barrett Browning's *Aurora Leigh*, but also in company with other writing women of her time, Phelps uses extraordinary means—diseases or physical wounds—to suggest the psychic deflation necessary to make men compatible with women.[13] That Phelps can so accept Myrton's behavior, as she had that of Emanuel Bayard—both characters deriving from her father's life—suggests the power her father held over her mind, even to the end of her career.

Whereas with *Walled In* Phelps contrasted two women central to the plot, in *Though Life Us Do Part* (1908), she returns to making central a contrast between two men.[14] The novel, serialized in *Women's Home Companion*, concerns the courtship and marriage of Cara Sterling, the last of Phelps's motherless young women. Like Avis and Marna, Cara marries an unstable man, who later philanders and then leaves her with a small child. Cara's cousin, the Reverend Sterling Hart, like Emanuel Bayard, assumes the duty of protecting Cara. His visit to her after her son's birth leaves him "sick at soul" from what he sees of her husband's callousness (106). Cara, however, never recognizes the depth of Sterling's devotion and seemingly takes it for granted.

Dr. Chaunceford Dane, the man to marry Cara, first gains her attention by attending her ailing father. He sees her as a "woman to make a man all he might be, and not to scorn him for what he was"—an echo of Philip Ostrander and Emanuel Bayard (69). Typically a suitor perceives not what he might offer a woman, but what she might do for him. After marriage, Chaunceford becomes enamored of a society patient and gradually succumbs to alcoholism. To avoid having to reveal his philandering, Chaunceford enlists in the Spanish-American war. Women, Phelps claims, are the worst victims of war: in America and Spain, "unconsulted women, who may not govern, who cannot fight—these give their happiness instead" (180).[15]

But Cara's happiness hardly develops. She finds herself "irresolute and troubled" in her love for Chaunceford—a love that feels like an undertow that might drown her (92). A war report indicates that Cara apparently has become a widow. She determines to earn her own living rather than accept her cousin's help; she becomes a businesswoman and a happy wage earner, themes absent from Phelps's work since "A Brave Girl" (1883).

But Cara's joy in self-management is short-lived. A renter of her husband's office turns out to be Chaunceford himself. Wishing not to spoil Cara's life a second time, Chaunceford conceals his identity in order to discover whether Cara still cares for him. In being considerate rather than self-absorbed, Chaunceford does penance for past unkindness. Though Cara wishes he had died rather than deserted her by concealing his identity, she willingly accepts him back. Once again, the institution of marriage survives intact, regardless of past or future human cost.

In *Though Life Us Do Part*, a title suggesting authorial valediction, Phelps has composed a coda to her life's work, since many of her favorite themes appear—namely, anti-alcoholism, anti-vivisection, women's self-support, men's demands upon women, and the problematic nature of courtship and marriage. In addition, over time Phelps recast her belief in women as support first for temperance and later for anti-vivisection. She thus modified her behavior away from acting in congruence with her deepest convictions about her own and other women's lives and placed her diminished energies behind related, though less personally involving, causes. In addition, she changed the basis of her argument for woman suffrage from human rights to female moral guardianship. Here was a process of "alienation from self": rather than continuing to act from the center of her being, Phelps gradually retreated from it and from her earlier advocacy of those women's issues more directly affecting her life.[16]

Career's End

The end of Phelps's career was typical of the whole—alternation between writing popular literature to produce income that would pay for a new house or new dress, and writing carefully crafted fiction for a serious audience.[17] The contrast between an assignment for *Harper's Bazar* and her magazine short stories makes clear Phelps's literary practice and her skillful versatility.

In 1907, the year before the publication of *Though Life Us Do Part*, she had participated in what was essentially a parlor game inflated into a magazine serialization—a novel called *The Whole Family*, written by twelve authors and serialized in *Harper's Bazar*. Correspondence between Phelps and *Bazar* editor Elizabeth Jordan (1865–1947) records Phelps's relation to the project. Each author wrote a chapter characterizing one member of "the whole family," beginning with "the father" by W. D. Howells followed by "the old-maid aunt" by M. E. Wilkins Freeman, and ending with the younger sister "Peggy" by Alice Brown and "the friend of the family" by H. van Dyke. Henry James's chapter, "The Married Son," immediately precedes Phelps's "The Married Daughter": two more oppositely oriented authors could not have been placed together! Phelps resented James's making a flirtatious aunt "vulgar" and determined that the married daughter's "being a manager" need not be an "aspersion," for such women, she claimed, are often the backbone of family life. Phelps must have felt gleeful as she registered her character Maria in New York City as a guest at "The Sphinx," "that nice ladies' hotel where mere man is never admitted" (192). Of course, "this is not literature," Phelps reminded Jordan.[18]

In contrast to this "strictly popular" writing, the short stories collected in *The Oath of Allegiance* (1909) and *The Empty House* (1910) showed more craft, ten of the twenty first appearing in *Harper's New Monthly* between 1893 and 1910. Eleven concern marriage, for the most part treated in stereotypic manner. Despite this fact, two from *The Empty House* merit separate mention for their autobiographical origin: "The Rejected Manuscript" (1893) depicts a woman's toil to seek a living from authorship; "The Romance of the Bill" (1902) shows a woman holding the attention of an uninterested committee by her knowledgeable testimony favoring "An Act Relative to the Rights of Mothers." In contrast to this independence, two stories from *Oath of Allegiance* depict self-sacrificing women: "The Autobiography of Aureola" (1904), who is too busy with the needs of others to worry about her own, and "The Chief Operator" (1909), who saves a town from flood waters but herself drowns. In each case, Phelps seems to advocate self-sacrifice as a satisfying stance in contrast to the feminine force of the two earlier stories. In these later stories married women have an edge over single women. Only three tales, all from *Oath of Allegiance*, consider such social issues as the dangers of an automobile in "Chariot of Fire" (1905; as gift book, 1910), the desperation of the "Unemployed" (1906), or the cruelty of vivisection in "Tammyshanty" (1908). "Jonathan and David" (*Harper's New Monthly*, 1904; gift book, 1909) also treats the relation between human and canine, but with emphasis upon mutual dependence rather than social wrong.[19]

Phelps's last short story, "Comrades" (1911), published posthumously in *Harper's New Monthly Magazine*, was one of her most successfully crafted stories.[20] The "comrades" of the title at first appear to be four Civil War veterans, but by the end Phelps makes very clear that veteran Reuben Oak's real comrade is his wife Patience. Three infirm veterans, expecting to "decorate" Reuben at the next Memorial Day celebration, die too soon. Reuben, kept alive by Patience's care, survives to "decorate" them instead. The last living survivor of his army post, Reuben realizes that Patience has been the "strength and warmth of his life" and tells her at last that she is "the best comrade of 'em all" (29, 31). Patience feels his words "worth the high cost of living" (32), but as they march together at the head of the Decoration Day parade, Phelps shows Patience embodying "all that blundering man has wrought on tormented women by the savagery of war" (39). Phelps questions whether the four veterans were "heroes" at all

(20). The real hero is Patience, actively nurturing the life around her; the alleged hero, Reuben, surviving only because of Patience's care, actually lives more passively than she. Not heroism but camaraderie counts in the long run of human survival: Phelps's last story affirms a woman's true strength, decries a man's false heroism.

When she died, Phelps was at work on a short story sequence in which she planned to treat "American urban life as shown in men's clubs of a certain sort." Ward later published this plan for "The Windsor Club Stories." The idea had originated at a luncheon given in 1889 by Annie Adams Fields and described in *Chapters from a Life*. Oliver Wendell Holmes—to Phillips Brook's cry that a certain Back Bay Boston men's club needed the preaching of the Salvation Army—had suggested, " 'But Doctor Brooks, such men as those are not going to listen to the Salvation Army. It seems to me that *you* are the man to go into the —Club, and preach Christianity' " (*Chapters*, 190-91). Although this idea never grew to fruition, it indicates Phelps's practice of settling upon circumstance long past as a story kernel.[21]

Never deeply analytical about the act of creation, she did hold convictions regarding artistic responsibility. In *Chapters from a Life* Phelps described her credo of "art for truth's sake." She held very high standards for the short story and found herself "often ill with the strain" of meeting her own "remorseless ... exaction" (*Chapters*, 267). She believed that the artist must "tell the truth about the world he [*sic*] lives in" (*Chapters*, 259). She found morality basic to any "truthful and conscientious study of life as it is" (*Chapters*, 261). But she added, " 'Helplessly to point the moral' is the last thing needful or artistic. The moral will take care of itself. Life is moral struggle. Portray the struggle, and you need write no tract" (*Chapters*, 264).

Her personal life during her last decade can only be hinted from extant correspondence. Three motifs permeate the letters: her solicitations for Ward's literary career, Ward's travels, and her own health. Though Phelps did what she could, Ward's literary career seems not to have prospered. By 1903 Phelps was no longer well enough to travel south with Ward for the winter.

It appears that he continued such mid-winter southern journeys without her. She once noted that she preferred such an arrangement, as it freed her mind from the anxiety that inhibited her writing. Apparently she preferred to have Ward away and happy, rather than home and restless. Certainly this was a reasonable and generous solution to potential conflict between her need to stay home because of her serious heart condition, known since 1903, and her husband's desire to winter in a southern climate, perhaps to benefit his own poor health.[22]

In February, 1903, Phelps had written to Spofford about calling in her letters because her heart condition had become serious.[23] She took a more serious turn at the beginning of January, 1911. She wrote her will twenty-six days before her death. In it she left to Ward the Newton house and the rest of her estate. On January 28, 1911, in the late afternoon, Elizabeth Stuart Phelps, then in her sixty-sixth year, died of myocardial degeneration. She had arranged for a longtime friend, Professor Leverett W. Spring, to assist at church services, and for her brother, the Reverend Lawrence Phelps, to conduct a brief service at the Mount Auburn Crematory. Her ashes were to be placed on a hillside in Newton Cemetery. They were to be marked by a headstone, carved with her name "Elizabeth Stuart Phelps Ward" and her own design of lilies, suggestive of her girlhood nickname Lily.

Chapter Six
Minor Work and Reputation

Elizabeth Stuart Phelps published fifty-seven volumes (three co-authored with Herbert Dickinson Ward) as well as two book-length serializations and numerous uncollected stories. She managed a successful and committed, if not distinguished, career as professional author. From 1868 until her death in 1911 she made the business of authorship her source of independence, frequently a personally unsatisfactory mode of gaining a livelihood, but nonetheless sufficiently lucrative for her to have amassed a reasonable estate by her death. In addition to the fiction that was her major work, she wrote plays, verse, essays, and biographies, which apparently her name as the popular "Gates" author made salable. Widely known during her lifetime, her name nearly faded from view upon her death. By the mid-1960s, however, her name reemerges with the inclusion in the John Harvard Library of *The Gates Ajar* and of *The Silent Partner* in the "Americans in Fiction Series." Circumstances in the 1960s similar to those of the 1860s account for revived interest in Phelps's fiction.[1]

Her Nonfiction

Verse and plays.   Of Phelps's two banal plays, never staged, one is *Within the Gates* (1901), a dramatization of *The Gates Between.* The other—*The Veteran: A Drama of the Street* appearing in *Pocket Magazine* (1895)—concerns a blind Civil War soldier, who through a technicality has not received a proper pension.

Phelps published two collections of verse, *Poetic Studies* (1875) and *Songs of the Silent World* (1884), neither of which merits particular attention—although the second contains several verses interesting for the restatement of themes treated in prose. Both are poetically undistinguished in that the lines show no distinctive rhymes or rhythms by twentieth-century standards, although Longfellow and Whittier found points to praise. Phelps's imagery is more interesting, especially when she creates a sense of place. Of the poems in the first volume, over half concern lost or unrequited love, a theme current in popular verse of her time but also likely to have personal basis in the death of Lt. Thompson. A fifth of the early verses treat a religious subject. Both of these themes appear in Phelps's second collection, again nearly half concerning love, about a fifth religion, and a substantial third occasional verses either memorializing such figures as Whittier, Stowe, Holmes, Longfellow, and George Eliot, or treating current issues such as women's needs ("The Sphinx" or "Victurae Salutamus"), fisherfolk's hardships ("Gloucester Harbor"), or commemoration of the Civil War dead ("Unseen Comrades"). Some uncollected verses still of interest are "Conemaugh," treating the Johnstown, Pennsylvania, flood of 1889, and "The Stone Woman of Eastern Point," again pleading the vulnerability of fisherfolk's lives.[2]

Essays and biographies. Three concerns emerge from this segment of Phelps's output—arguing for immortality, memorializing those close to her, and addressing social wrongs. From the last concern, only one book on women's dress (*What to Wear?* [1873]) and five pamphlets resulted: the pamphlets are addresses on anti-vivisection, delivered before Massachusetts legislative committees, 1901-1903. Numerous uncollected essays representing a spectrum of ills experienced by women and the poor appeared over four decades in the *Century, Harper's Monthly, Harper's Bazar*, the *Independent*, and the *Woman's Journal*. Her own autobiography *Chapters from a Life* is part collected essays, part fresh reminiscence: since friends mentioned were deceased, she had previously published prose memorials to James T. Fields, Edward Rowland Sill, John Greenleaf Whittier, Phillips Brooks, and Lucy Larcom, as well as a discussion of *The Gates Ajar* viewed from a retrospective vantage-point of twenty-five years. She also memorialized her stepmother's mother in the 1888 booklet *A Gracious Life* and her father in *Austin Phelps: A*

Memoir (1891), the latter notable for hardly mentioning the man's daughter.[3]

Her religious concern for immortality, as in the "Gates" series, appears to derive from a concern for righting wrongs to the weak, especially to women. *The Struggle for Immortality* (1889) collected essays which had appeared in the *Atlantic Monthly*, *Forum*, and *North American Review*. Such essays, though today unbelievable, do reveal severe malaise. Her latest essay on the subject, in 1908, included the following reassurance to women:

These biographies of famine, these histories of denied capacity, are pathetically numerous among women—the simple, domestic women, householding, homekeeping, the wives of husbands, the mothers of children. No woman who has ever received the confidences of her sex can recall without emotion the confessions of these gentle and unhoping spirits, tied to traditions which they dare not question, broken on the wheels of drudgery whose iron revolutions crush individual gifts out of the soul, and personal powers out of the life. I am quite willing to suggest it as my belief that "the judgment of Eve" will be one of the first tragedies which another life will recognize, and rectify; and that there will be no happier class of citizens in the heavenly country than the prisoners of sex to whom the unlocked door of death has given the freedom of their own natures.[4]

Undertaken at S. S. McClure's request, her 1897 *The Story of Jesus Christ: An Interpretation*, in which Phelps was "not interested in academic or scholarly details of the life," explicates Jesus as the ideal Friend of woman: He was respectful, forgiving, cognizant of her "fettered individualism," "undeveloped powers," and "superiority in spiritual vigor." One of the constraints upon Phelps's life was that, unlike Elizabeth Cady Stanton and her *Woman's Bible* committee, Phelps never understood the contradiction inherent in Christian belief—that solely male divinity and authority are incompatible with human fulfillment, especially when female. Because Phelps saw so little of such fulfillment in this life, she required another as compensation: only so could she justify the misery of this world.[5]

Her Contemporary Stature

Phelps wrote fifteen works of juvenile fiction, plus sundry uncollected contributions appearing first in *Our Young Folks*, *St. Nicholas*, *Youth's Companion*, and *Wide Awake*, major youth magazines of the era, as well as in the *Woman's Journal*. As noted, the juvenile works were part of her apprentice period of the 1860s and her middle period of strong female portrayals during the 1870s and 1880s. Only two juvenile works appeared during the 1890s, one being *A Lost Hero* (1891), co-authored with Ward. Her lively and appealing portrayals for youth follow the major plot formulas of her era: the ordeal of separation, isolation, and reintegration, often of a heroine; the change of heart believed necessary to moral growth, usually a hero's ; or its variation, the gentry mission of causing such change in another, often a heroine's in her brother or his friend. Save for Whittier's approval of "A Brave Girl" noted earlier, critical responses to the juvenilia appear not to have survived.[6]

Her short stories, five volumes collected primarily from the *Atlantic*, *Century*, *Harper's Bazar*, *Harper's New Monthly*, *Independent*, and *Scribner's*—again the major monthlies of their type—show her range of social concerns and her often skilled execution. Whereas her short story publication in the *Atlantic* peaked during the 1860s, her appearance in *Harper's Monthly* was continuous. In addition, seven tales appear in individual, illustrated gift editions.[7] Her first collection—*Men, Women, and Ghosts* (1879)—contains "The Tenth of January," the 1868 realistic tale that launched her serious literary career by bringing her to Higginson's and Whittier's attention. The next—*Sealed Orders* (1880)—elicited praise from Oliver Wendell Holmes and Whittier, the latter comparing it to Hawthorne's *Twice-Told Tales* while the *Literary World* found its realism similar to the work of Bret Harte.[8] Not until 1891 did Phelps bring out *Fourteen to One*, including "Madonna of the Tubs" and "Jack," each of which received independent critical review. Whittier considered "Madonna" her "best story." The half dozen extant reviews without exception praise Phelps's characterization of the laundress: for instance, the London *Saturday Review* found that the fisherfolk vocabulary "resonates." Holmes found "Jack" a great story and the *Nation* claimed it on a level with the realism of George Eliot or Tolstoy. The collection as a whole the *Atlantic* considered to exhibit artful construction tied to human action.[9] This Phelps collection elicited more acclaim than any other. *Oath of Allegiance* (1909) received small attention: *Saturday Review* and *Nation* compared it to Mary W. Freeman and Louisa May Alcott, respectively.[10] Finally, *The Empty House* (1910), offering no themes not appearing in her novels, seems to have passed unnoticed. Many uncollected stories feature situations favorable to women, such as "Zerviah Hope," a tale praised by Whittier for its depiction of female physician and male nurse.[11]

Although Phelps's contemporaries sometimes placed equal value upon her stories, her novels are the work upon which her reputation rests, then as now. Obituary notices regularly cited novels: the *New York Times* listed "noted works" as *Avis*, *Friends*, or *Doctor Zay* while the *Independent* favored *Avis*, *Madonna of the Tubs*, and *A Singular Life*. This review placed her at the head of American women authors and noted her early maturity in that *The Gates Ajar* appeared when she was twenty-four. Interestingly, given her concern for women, the *Woman's Journal* printed only a photograph of Phelps with two pet dogs, accompanied by a memorial verse, but made no comment upon her authorship. A *Boston Transcript* article did emphasize Phelps's concern for women and stressed *Avis* and *A Singular Life* as her masterworks.[12]

During her lifetime Phelps's novels received regular notice. Since *Silent Partner*, *Avis*, *Doctor Zay*, and *A Singular Life* represent her best work but have received less attention than her "Gates" series, discussing critical responses to these four works may be most helpful. Perhaps because following most closely after *The Gates Ajar*, even more popular in England than the United States, *Silent Partner* received London notices, the *Saturday Review* commenting upon its "mannered style" and noting the influence of *Mill on the Floss*, the *Athenaeum* praising the characterization of Perley and finding occasional eloquence.

Harper's Monthly disliked the bad imitation of Dickens and unnatural conclusion but found it overall "effective and artistic," a "lesson for capital to ponder," while *Literary World*, also faulting an "extravagant style" and "abrupt" end, praised its superior realism and the contrasting characterizations of Perley and Sip.[13]

Critics were less comfortable with *Avis*, though they generally recognized its iconoclastic content and Phelps's skill and strength as an author. *Harper's* found it unwholesome as well as inappropriate for young girls, and held that though Phelps may have seen into a woman's heart, she made the man unnaturally weak. The *Nation* suggested that *Middlemarch* inspired *Avis* (but was stylistically superior) and complained of the "monotony of unrelieved misery" even though it revealed "rarely expressed truth." *Literary World* noted Phelps's continued extravagant language, but labelled her one of the "masters of modern fiction" in having created a "most notable American product of its class in many years." Lucy Stone, editor of the *Woman's Journal*, predicted a "permanent place in English Literature" for *Avis* and praised the delineation of character; a later *Journal* article rebutted widespread criticism to find *Avis*'s strengths in theme and character surpassing its faults. Longfellow and Whittier, as well as juvenile biographer Sarah Knowles Bolton (1841–1916), wrote to Phelps praising *Avis*.[14]

Responses to *Doctor Zay* reveal more about critics' attitudes toward women than about their estimate of its literary quality. The *Critic* found the novel balancing purpose and humor with sentiment but ending abruptly, thus not solving the problem of the marriage in process; the reviewer contrasts *Doctor Zay* with *Avis*, "one of the remarkable novels of our generation," where painting could more easily be integrated into marriage than medicine. The *Independent* praised the style, admired Zay as an exceptional model, but criticized Phelps's marriage theory for inadequately recognizing marital provision of happiness. *Literary World* declared *Doctor Zay* "readable but not great" and predicted Yorke would have been unable to share his "own peculiar treasure" with her patients. By contrast, a *Woman's*

Journal article wished Phelps had provided Zay a stronger man more worthy of her choices and conquest than Yorke. Whittier found *Doctor Zay* the "best book of the season" and Lucy Larcom (1829–1893), though she found it one of Phelps's "strongest," would rather Zay had not married.[15]

Not surprisingly, the more conservative *A Singular Life* received widespread praise. Reviews in the *Dial*, *Literary World*, and *Woman's Journal* recognized religious sources in the recent Andover controversy over "applied" versus "doctrinal" religion. The *World* believed only a woman could have imagined such a hero, while the *Dial* and *Journal* considered this Phelps's best work yet. The *Independent* concurred that *A Singular Life* was "one of the strongest of recent novels," but the *Dial* found it "marred by a note of hysterical emotion." And while a member of the Essex County bar (in a sixteen-page booklet) scolded Phelps for defaming the city of Gloucester in the Windover of *A Singular Life*, sales for the book showed her public enthusiastic.[16]

The critic T. W. Higginson, in an 1871 overview of "Late Books by American Women," considered Phelps a writer of "more genius" than either Alcott or Stowe, but noted that she "is led on by her own fiery earnestness, and intense purpose to a similar disregard of literary execution." But in 1884 the poet Edward Rowland Sill reported lecturing favorably on Barrett Browning and Phelps as "exemplifying the characteristic *pity* of our age—the pitifulness of those who never had a chance." In 1887 a letter to the *Woman's Journal* claimed Phelps, not William Dean Howells, to be the "greatest novelist" in America because she wakes up her readers and writes literature "of tomorrow." Some years later Willa Cather would dub Howells the "young ladies' illusion preserver," corroboration of the lulling effect the *Journal* correspondent attributed to him. Not surprisingly Phelps had requested that Howells not be asked to review *Silent Partner*, since she felt he would be uninterested. As in more recent criticism, some favored Phelps for her content, others chastised her for her style, each according to individual taste. But whatever their views, her name was known nationally and internationally: Montgomery Ward & Co., in its 1895 catalog, lists her "Gates" and "Gypsy" books, confident of their salability, and German author of travel guides Karl Baedeker in his 1893 *United States* notes that Gloucester is the location of Phelps's "summer-house (see her 'Old Maid's Paradise')" and that she wrote *The Gates Ajar* in Andover's Phelps House.[17]

Revitalization of a Reputation

Although Phelps appears frequently in literary studies completed during the 1930s and early 1940s, she gains significant attention only in the mid-1960s, after which her appearances outnumber all previous considerations. Like her contemporaries, modern critics continue to find her content compelling, her style problematic: which trait a given critic emphasizes varies with prevailing critical theory or individual persuasion.

Fred Lewis Pattee, in *A History of American Literature since 1870* (1915), places Phelps among such "recorders of New England decline" as Sarah Orne Jewett, Mary Wilkins Freeman, and Alice Brown. Appearing four years after her death, this study summarizes contemporary critical views. Pattee finds *The Gates Ajar* to have significance beyond literary merit as a *journal intime* of a woman trying to reconcile Puritan doctrine with her own emotional desolation. He emphasizes the autobiographical nature of all of her work, but finds that the preacher in her dominated the novelist. He finds successful realism in the stories "Madonna of the Tubs," "Jack the Fisherman," and "The Supply at St. Agatha's." He misses the Utopian, social dimension of Phelps's "Gates" books and omits what most have considered to be her major novels, but otherwise his is a typical estimate.[18]

V. L. Parrington, in *The Beginnings of Critical Realism in America: 1860–1920* (1930, the third volume of his *Main Currents in American Thought*), considers *The Silent Partner* the first novel to criticize New England industrialism, but scorns it as "an emotional Puritan document that was out of date when it came to the press" because of basing justice upon "understanding and Christian kindliness" (62). He finds Freeman's *The Portion of Labor* (1901) more adequate. Surely Phelps was limited by her

Christian viewpoint, but her novel makes clearer than Freeman's the portion of woman as partner or laborer. Parrington ignores the fifty-six remaining volumes Phelps published.[19]

Arthur Hobson Quinn, on the other hand, in *American Fiction: An Historical and Critical Survey* (1936), provides the most complete overview of Phelps contained within a survey. Attributing the popularity of *The Gates Ajar* to its consolatory message, he stresses Phelps's humanization of a superhuman heaven. He finds *The Silent Partner* unsurpassed in its best scenes save by Dickens. He contrasts *The Story of Avis* with Henry James's *Roderick Hudson* (1875), noting Phelps's creation of an artist who surmounts duress while James's male artist succumbs. Likewise, Quinn prefers Phelps's *Doctor Zay* to Howells's *Dr. Breen's Practice* (1881). He finds *A Singular Life* her masterpiece and praises its love story and portrait of a woman. Quinn's discussion is complete and fair. We might stress more than he Phelps's secularization of religion and her constant concern for women's issues, but he places her within the context of her contemporaries to strengthen rather than diminish her stature.[20]

More than Quinn, Van Wyck Brooks in *New England: Indian Summer 1865–1915* (1940) places Phelps within a broad, historical-cultural context. He rightly sees hers as "problem stories," accurately lists "dress reform, anti-vivisection, woman's rights and other humanitarian themes" as her causes, but finds her "too consciously righteous." He places her among the first to study slums in *Hedged In* and *The Silent Partner*. He compares Avis to Hilda of Hawthorne's *Marble Faun* (1860), but misunderstands Phelps to mean that the art career is wrecked by an invalid husband and could properly succeed only if a woman remains single![21]

In contrast to Quinn and Brooks, Quinn's student Mary Angela Bennett is less fully sympathetic. Hers is the first full-length study, *Elizabeth Stuart Phelps* (1939). It contains the exhaustive bibliography of published work, missing only Phelps's *Woman's Journal* contributions. Bennett's coverage is thorough, if factual rather than interpretive, but she underplays Phelps's strong feminist sympathies and emphasis upon women's issues. In addition, she fails to recognize the incisiveness of Phelps's challenge to patriarchy. The author of a 1950 dissertation, including Phelps's work among those examined, deliberately refuses to analyze from a feminist viewpoint. Given the 1950s "feminine mystique" and New Criticism's hostility not only to women but to social issues in general, perhaps we should be surprised this dissertation exists at all.[22]

Where previous studies place Phelps in a literary, broadly cultural, or social-critical context, James D. Hart in *The Popular Book* (1950) places the *The Gates Ajar* within the context of American popular reading taste, specifically the popular mid-nineteenth-century thesis novel having a religious concern. He calculates that all her "Gates" books were widely read in the years immediately following their publication.[23] After this study Phelps drops from sight until a 1964 reprinting of her most popular book.

Helen Sootin Smith, with her important Introduction to the John Harvard Library edition of *The Gates Ajar* (1964), begins a new era of concern for Phelps. Hers is a thorough religious, biographical, and literary analysis of this book and its origins, not to be omitted by any serious student of Phelps, since she raises major critical issues. Smith misses several small points, however: Phelps's health probably resulted from her feminist stance as well as her family's behavior patterns (xvi); the sister-brother relation in *The Gates Ajar* need not be interpreted as sublimated incest but as Phelps's recasting of Thompson's death (xvi); contrary to Smith's assertion, Phelps did question "larger social and economic forces" in her feminist essays (xx). Smith rightly perceives Phelps's heaven as "a Utopian analogue of the world she knew" (xxi), points to the shaping force of Phelps's family upon her work, and stresses Phelps's unflinching feminism.[24]

Three other researchers place the "Gates" books at the center of Phelps's output. The historian Barbara Welter in "Defenders of the Faith" (1976) stresses Phelps's Utopian feminist view. Welter discusses not only the "Gates" books but also her prose writing on religion, as well as *A Singular Life, Avis, Doctor Zay*, and *Confessions of a Wife*. She sees the latter three novels depicting the earthly correlate of the heavenly "Gates" work and *A Singular Life* depicting religious changes that would make men fit to live in a world with women. In his study "Paradise Deferred: The Image of Heaven in the Work of Emily Dickinson and Elizabeth Stuart Phelps" (1977), literary critic Barton Levi St. Armand discusses *Gates Ajar* as making explicit the views of heaven which are implicit in Emily Dickinson's poetry. (St. Armand repeats an error of Dickinson's editors Johnson and Ward in labelling Phelps an editor of the *Woman's Journal*: she was of course an "occasional contributor.") St. Armand finds the "personal fulfillment" not possible on earth deferred to a Utopian heaven. Finally, American studies scholar Ann Douglas in *The Feminization of American Culture* (1977) sees the "Gates" books as both offers of a consolatory compensation and as bids to dominate instead of being dominated.[25]

Equal in importance to interpreting the "Gates" books is considering Phelps's feminism. In "Elizabeth Stuart Phelps: A Study in Female Rebellion" (1972), Christine Stansell treats *Gates Ajar, Avis, Doctor Zay,* and *Old Maid's Paradise,* which she weaves into a careful discussion of the relationship between feminist rebellion, as expressed in the literature, and lifelong invalidism. Ann Douglas Wood further develops the invalidism in " 'The Fashionable Diseases': Women's Complaints and their Treatment in Nineteenth-Century America" (1973) with reference to *Doctor Zay,* in which she sees medicine as a "weapon in a social and political struggle for power between the sexes." Also examining *Doctor Zay,* Alfred Habegger, in "Nineteenth-Century American Humor: Easygoing Males, Anxious Ladies, and Penelope Lapham" (1976), cites a minor humorous figure, Mrs. Butterwell, as a mouthpiece of feminist sagacity: he might also have included Puelvir of the "Paradise" series.[26]

Another central consideration is Phelps's depiction of the woman artist in *The Story of Avis.* Lee R. Edwards and Arlyn Diamond in their introduction to *American Voices, American Women* (1973) emphasize the conflict between love and domesticity versus art, while Grace Stewart in "Mother, Daughter, and the Birth of the Female Artist" stresses the problematic nature of the mother-daughter relation in the development of a woman artist.[27]

Three holistic and complementary studies of Phelps's life and work are complete: Susan Margaret Coultrap-McQuin, "Elizabeth Stuart Phelps: The Cultural Context of a Nineteenth-Century Professional Writer"; Lori Duin Kelly, "'Oh the Poor Women!': A Study of Elizabeth Stuart Phelps"; and my own "'The Woman's Hour': Life and Novels of Elizabeth Stuart Phelps, 1844-1911."[28]

In a talk entitled "Those We Still Don't Read," Florence Howe listed *The Silent Partner*, *The Story of Avis*, and *Doctor Zay* as works that merit availability.[29] Of these only *Partner* is available in a reasonably priced edition; *Avis* appears in excerpt or in expensive reprint, *Doctor Zay* not at all. Phelps's work, from being internationally known, has nearly disappeared. But slowly with a revitalized women's movement and burgeoning women's studies research, Elizabeth Stuart Phelps and her work are being reclaimed, particularly because she did place foremost in her work the study of women's lives.

No doubt exists regarding Phelps's innovative capacity as a writer: she made religious literature into feminist Utopia, first treated seriously the problems of urban industrialization, and perhaps more outspokenly than any other contemporary American author challenged relations between the sexes. But for us all her style has remained a source of difficulty: why wasn't she more careful? more controlled? less contorted? How can we explain what appears as lack of attention in a writer so earnest in her commitment to write effectively? Perhaps our questions are wrong. We need recall that if self-doubt can silence a writer, surely it could also roughen the surface of what writing she accomplishes. Stylistic grace may well rest as much upon self-assurance as upon conscious care. Contrast *Avis* and *A Singular Life* stylistically. *Avis*, presenting views in conflict with cultural assumptions regarding gender roles, seems written as if Phelps searched for the *mot juste*, the graceful phrase, but had difficulty finding either; *A Singular Life*, on the other hand, not questioning gender relationships, seems more gracefully expressed.

Even though her work provides no model of stylistic excellence, nonetheless her social content was ahead of her time. She saw clearly the depth of the chasm between women and men and creatively imagined alternative modes of living as relief. Perhaps the social imagination in literature is as worthy of study as the verbal or stylistic.

Phelps's life was the source of her need to write, the writing her answer to life's insoluble problems. Paternal "feudal views" regarding women's needs and capacities early set a limit upon her. Family patterns of psychological anxiety informing such beliefs continued into her own life. The "dual nature" she recognized in her mother—the capacity to nurture and the need to achieve—she depicted in her own work, felt divided by in her life. A partial resolution lay in following her mother's unfulfilled career of authorship, however doubting she was about her own abilities.

Given life's deprivations, Phelps imagined in her popular "Gates" books a Utopian heaven where women and the poor might find the satisfaction and fulfillment earth had withheld. In her realistic fiction she revealed the constraints upon women's earthly lives—sexual, occupational, marital, emotional. Even though home then stood in people's minds just below heaven as a refuge from a world in flux, Phelps's fictional homes are typically not happy. In transposing some facts of her own biography into the "Paradise" set, she publicized ways women might assert control over their lives, and in fiction for girls she advocated preparation for self-dependence.

But her life's losses seem finally to have overwhelmed her. Deaths of friends and family, increasing invalidism expressed as incurable insomnia, neuralgia, and paralysis, reduced her power. Her father's view that a woman be submissive, her mother's that a woman accomplish, so pulled her in opposite directions as to render her an invalid unable to continue in her mother's footsteps.

The genius was in Elizabeth Stuart Phelps, as in her mother.[30] We regret that social conditions prevented its fulfillment in work stylistically as well as socially superior, but nonetheless we admire her fearless example of depicting socially threatening dilemmas and suggesting revolutionary answers. The words of her contemporary John Greenleaf Whittier aptly encapsulate Phelps's personality—"an intense nature—frail but strong—a Puritan with the passion and fire of Sappho and the moral courage of Joan of Arc."[31]

Notes and References

Chapter One

1. *Chapters from a Life* (Boston, 1896), p. 24; hereafter cited in the text as *Chapters*, followed by page number.

2. Mrs. S[arah] S[tuart] Robbins, *Old Andover Days* (Boston: Pilgrim Press, 1909), p. 164.

3. Robbins, *Old Andover Days*, p. 176; Harriet Beecher Stowe, "Lines on the Death of Mrs. Professor Stuart" in *Religious Poems* (Boston: Ticknor and Fields, 1867), pp. 54-55.

4. On insomnia, see Karen Horney, *Neurosis and Human Growth: The Struggle toward Self-Realization* (New York: W. W. Norton & Co., 1950), pp. 233-34. On the Phelps patterns of illness as culturally sanctioned ways of dealing with repression, see Helen Sootin Smith, Introduction to *The Gates Ajar* (Cambridge, Mass., 1964), p. xiv. On moral philosophy, see D[onald] H. Meyer, *The Instructed Conscience: The Shaping of the American National Ethic* (Philadelphia: University of Pennsylvania Press, 1974).

5. Quoted by Meyer, *Instructed Conscience*, p. 80.

6. Horney, *Neurosis*, pp. 13, 64-65.

7. Bernard J. Paris, *A Psychological Approach to Fiction: A Study in Thackeray, Stendhal, George Eliot, Dostoevsky, and Conrad* (Bloomington: University of Indiana Press, 1974), esp. p. 279; p. 299, n5.

8. Robbins, *Old Andover Days*, pp. 67, 87.

9. Quoted by Austin Phelps, "A Memorial of the Author" in *The Last Leaf from Sunny Side*, H. Trusta [pseud.], (Boston: Phillips, Sampson, 1853), p. 18.

10. Mother quoted by A. Phelps, "A Memorial," p. 94. For daughter's relation to father, see letters to John Greenleaf Whittier, Mar. 13, 1868, Houghton Library, Harvard University, and to William Dean Howells, June 29, 1874, Rutherford B. Hayes Library, Fremont, Ohio; "The Man Who Most Influenced Me," *Ladies Home Journal* 12 (May, 1885):2.

11. For the daughter's view, see Julia Ward Howe, ed., *Sex and Education: A Reply to Dr. E. H. Clarke's "Sex in Education,"* (Boston, 1874), chap. 7.

12. Quoted by A. Phelps, "A Memorial," pp. 37-38.

13. Smith, Introduction to *The Gates Ajar*, p. xiv.

14. Carroll Smith-Rosenberg, "The Hysterical Woman: Sex Roles and Role Conflict in Nineteenth Century America," *Social Research* 39 (1972):677-78.

15. *Austin Phelps: A Memoir* (New York, 1891), pp. 51, 56; hereafter cited in text as *A. Phelps* followed by page number.

16. Quotes from Austin Phelps, "A Pastor of the Last Generation," a three-part memorial in *My Portfolio* (New York: Scribner's, 1882), pp. 3, 9, 10.

17. Philip Slater, *The Pursuit of Loneliness: American Culture at the Breaking Point* (Boston: Beacon Press, 1970), chap. 3, esp. p. 74.

18. A. Phelps, "Pastor," p. 29.

19. A. Phelps, "Memorial," pp. 53, 73-74.

20. H. Trusta [pseud.], *Little Mary; or Talks and Tales for Children* (Boston: Phillips, Sampson, 1854), p. 117.

21. Tillie Olsen, *Silences* (New York: Delta Press, 1978), p. 10.

22. James D. Hart, *The Popular Book* (New York: Oxford University Press, 1950), p. 111.

23. A. Phelps, "Memorial," p. 84.

24. [Elizabeth Stuart Phelps], *Angel Over the Right Shoulder* (1852; rpt. in Mary Anne Ferguson, ed., *Images of Women in Literature*, 3rd ed., Boston: Houghton Mifflin, 1981), pp. 35-36; hereafter page references cited in the text. Parts of the following discussion previously appeared in *Frontiers: A Journal of Women Studies* 5, no. 3 (Fall 1980):28-33.

25. For convention, see Walter E. Houghton, *The Victorian Frame of Mind, 1830-1870* (New Haven: Yale University Press, 1957), chap. 13, esp. pp. 341-48.

26. Quoted by A. Phelps, "Memorial," p. 90.

27. A. Phelps, "Memorial," pp. 92-93.

28. For examples, Mary Angela Bennett, *Elizabeth Stuart Phelps* (Philadelphia, 1939); *A Woman of the Century: 1470 Biographical Sketches...* (Boston: C. W. Moulton, 1893), s.v. "Ward, Elizabeth Stuart Phelps"; Hervis Kay, clipping in Scrapbook, "E.S. Phelps, 1878," Clifton Waller Barrett Library, University of Virginia.

29. Ella Gilbert Ives, "Elizabeth Stuart P. Ward," *Boston Transcript*, Feb. 4, 1911.

30. Ibid.

31. Charlotte Porter and Helen A. Clarke, eds., *The Complete Works of Elizabeth Barrett Browning*, vols. 4 & 5: *Aurora Leigh* (1900; rpt. New York: AMS, 1973).

Chapter Two

1. Mark Holloway, *Heavens on Earth: Utopian Communities in America, 1680–1880* (New York: Dover, 1962), pp. 160-224.

2. Kenneth M. Roemer, *The Obsolete Necessity: America in Utopian Writings, 1888–1900* (Kent, Ohio: Kent State University Press, 1976), pp. 124-33.

3. Information concerning this relationship appears in Bennett, *Elizabeth Stuart Phelps*; Ella Gilbert Ives, "Elizabeth Stuart P. Ward," *Boston Transcript*, Feb. 4, 1911; photo in *McClure's* 6 (Mar. 1896):362.

4. It is worth noting that over half the poems in Phelps's *Poetic Studies* (Boston, 1875) concern a lost love, the loss frequently occurring through death.

5. Elizabeth Stuart Phelps in *Sex and Education*, Julia Ward Howe, ed., chap. 7, pp. 126-38; hereafter cited in text as *Sex* followed by page number.

6. "A Sacrifice Consumed," *Harper's New Monthly Magazine* 28 (Jan., 1864):240.

7. *Ellen's Idol* (Boston, 1864); *Tiny* (Boston, 1864); *Tiny's Sunday Nights* (Boston, 1866); *I Don't Know How* (Boston, 1867).

8. *Gypsy Breynton, Gypsy's Cousin Joy, Gypsy's Sowing and Reaping,* (Boston, 1866), *Gypsy's Year at the Golden Crescent* (Boston, 1867).

9. *Mercy Gliddon's Work* (Boston, 1865); hereafter cited in text as *Mercy* followed by page number.

10. Austin Phelps, "Memorial," pp. 97, 99.

11. *Up Hill; or Life in the Factory* (Boston, 1865); hereafter page references cited in the text.

12. "Jane Gurley's Story," *Hours at Home* 2 (Mar.-Apr., 1866) and 3 (May-Oct., 1866); hereafter volume and page references cited in the text.

13. *The Gates Ajar*, editorial note by Helen Sootin Smith (1868; rpt. Cambridge, 1964), p. 53.

14. Alice C. Crozier, *The Novels of Harriet Beecher Stowe* (New York: Oxford, 1969), pp. 94-97.

15. Bennett, *Elizabeth Stuart Phelps*, pp. 50-52, discusses contemporary clerical responses to *The Gates Ajar*; see also *McClure's Magazine*, 6 (May, 1896):515.

16. On sequels, see Phelps to Francis Jackson Garrison, July 26, 1883, Beinecke Rare Book and Manuscript Library, Yale University.

17. On plan, see Phelps to H. O. Houghton, Sept. 28, 1883, Houghton Library, Harvard University; *Beyond the Gates* (Boston, 1883); hereafter page references cited in the text.

18. Phelps to "My dear friend" [John Greenleaf Whittier], May 14, 1882, Alderman Library, University of Virginia.

19. Quoted by Barbara Cross, ed., *The Educated Woman in America* (New York: Teachers' College Press, 1965), pp. 29-30.

20. *The Gates Between* (Boston, 1887); hereafter page references cited in the text.

21. *The Woman's Journal* 18 (Oct., 1887):32.

22. For examples of authors known to Phelps who used this device of otherworldly communication, see Margaret Oliphant (1828–1897), *A Little Pilgrim in the Unseen* (1882); and Harriet Prescott Spofford, "The Amber Gods," *Atlantic* 5 (1860), rpt. Lee R. Edwards and A. Diamond, eds., *American Voices, American Women* (New York: Avon Books, 1973), pp. 21-62. Spofford's main character narrated her life from the perspective of her death. Phelps cited this story as one that had had a "subtle influence" upon the direction of her work in "Stories That Stay," *Century* 59 (Nov., 1910) :119.

23. *Within the Gates* (Boston, 1901). The title repeats one used by Whittier for a memorial to Lydia Marie Child (1802-1880), "Within the Gates"; see letter to Whittier, Mar. 8, 1881, Houghton Library, Harvard University. The play was first published in *McClure's Magazine* 17 (May-July, 1901). For changed expectations of staging the play, see letters to H. O. Houghton (Nov. 23, [1895], Houghton Library, Harvard University), and to Elizabeth Garver Jordan (Apr. 9 and 11, 1900, Manuscripts and Archives Division, New York Public Library).

24. Northrup Frye, "Varieties of Literary Utopias" in Frank E. Manuel, ed., *Utopias and Utopian Thought* (Boston: Houghton, Mifflin, 1966), p. 32.

25. Margaret Oliphant, *Blackwood's Magazine* 10 (Oct., 1871): 422-42, quoted by Smith, *The Gates Ajar*, p. xxiii, n. 22.

26. Phelps's comment on invalidism, quoated by Bennett, *Phelps*, p. 63; "What Shall They Do?" *Harper's New Monthly Magazine* 35 (Sept. 1867): 519-23.

27. "Why Shall They Do It?" *Harper's New Monthly Magazine* 36 (Jan. 1868): 218-23.

28. "The Tenth of January," *Atlantic Monthly* 21 (Mar. 1868); the story was collected in *Men, Women, and Ghosts* (Boston, 1869).

29. Letters from Whittier indicate his response to "Gates" books: on Dec. 27, [1883] he found *Beyond the Gates* better than *The Gates Ajar*; on Sept. 23, 1887, he wrote that *The Gates Between* (he called it by the 1883 title!) was "the best of thy wonderful series" and noted on Nov. 18, 1887 that the book would "do immense Good" (all letters, Friends Historical Library, Swarthmore College). On July 26, 1883, however, Phelps was not sure that Whittier would want to say publicly that he liked *Beyond the Gates* (Phelps to Francis Jackson Garrison, Beinecke Rare Book and Manuscript Library, Yale University). Her uncertainty suggests that Whittier's approval was more personal than public, an approval designed to gain from her reciprocal approval for himself rather than to make a statement about her work.

Chapter Three

1. From "Victurae Salutamus" in Phelps's *Songs of the Silent World and Other Poems* (Boston, 1885), p. 99.

2. "The Gist of the Matter," *Woman's Journal* 2 (July 22, 1871), reprinted from *Independent* 23 (July 13, 1871).

3. Most articles appeared in *Independent* (*In*) 23 (1871) and/or *Woman's Journal* (*WJ*) 2 (1871): "Where It Goes," *In* July 20; "Unhappy Girls," *In* July 27; *WJ* Aug. 12; "Too Much Conscience," *In* Aug. 3; *WJ* Aug. 19; "Song of the Shirt," *In* Aug. 10; *WJ* Sept. 2; "What They Are Doing," *In* Aug. 17; "Women and Money," *In* Aug. 24; "Men and Muscle," *In* Aug. 31; "Rights and Relatives," *In* Sept. 7; *WJ* Sept. 23; "'The United Head,'" *In* Sept. 14; *WJ* Sept. 30; "The New Earth," *In* Sept. 28; "The Higher Claim," *In* Oct. 5; *WJ* Oct. 28; "'The True Woman,'" *In* Oct. 10. Other articles appeared in *In* 24 (1872) and/or *WJ* 3 (1872): "A Talk to Girls," *In* Jan. 4; *WJ* Jan. 27; "A Few Words to the Girls," *WJ* Feb. 24. *Woman's Journal* appears in the microfilm collection *History of Women: A Comprehensive Collection . . .* (Woodbridge, Conn.: Research Publications, Inc). *Independent* is collected on microfilm in *American Periodicals, 1800–1850*, Years 38-42 (Ann Arbor: University Microfilms, 1976).

4. *Hedged In* (Boston, 1870); hereafter page references cited in the text.

5. *The Silent Partner* (Boston, 1871); hereafter page references cited in the text. On recommending business, see *Harper's New Monthly Magazine* 36 (Jan., 1868) and *Independent* 24 (Jan. 4, 1872).

6. Phelps to [James Ripley] Osgood, May 13, 1871, Houghton Library, Harvard University.

7. See studies by Van Wyck Brooks, *New England: Indian Summer 1865-1915* (New York: Dutton, 1940); Claude R. Flory, *The Economic Novel in American Fiction 1792-1900* (Philadelphia: University of Pennsylvania Press, 1936); Gordon Milne, *The American Political Novel* (Norman: University of Oklahoma Press, 1966); Vernon L. Parrington, Jr., *Main Currents of American Thought*, Vol. 3: *The Beginnings of Critical Realism in America: 1860-1920* (New York: Harcourt, 1930); Walter F. Taylor, *The Economic Novel in America* (Chapel Hill: University of North Carolina Press, 1942).

8. "Stories That Stay," *Century Magazine* 59 (Nov., 1910): 120; Rebecca Harding Davis, *Life in the Iron Mills* (Old Westbury: Feminist Press, 1972).

9. R. Rosen and S. Davidson, eds. *The Maimie Papers*, (Old Westbury: Feminist Press, 1977).

10. Phelps [Ward] to "Dear Sir," Jan. 15, 1873, Massachusetts Historical Society.

11. Phelps [Ward] to A[bby] W. May, May 25, 1876, Schlesinger Library, Radcliffe College.

12. Phelps [Ward] to A[bby] W. May, Jan. 23, 1873, Schlesinger Library, Radcliffe College.

13. *What to Wear?* (Boston, 1873); references in text are to the book. "Woman's Dress," *Independent* 22 (May 1, 8, 15, 22, 1873).

14. On Phelps's dress views, see Madeleine Stern, *Lousia May Alcott* (Norman: University of Oklahoma Press, 1950), p. 233; *Woman's Journal* 4 (1873), esp. Sept. 20, 1873:300.

15. "The 'Female Education' of Women," *Independent* 25 (Nov. 13, 1873); reprinted in *Woman's Journal* 4 (Nov. 22, 1873); see also "The Experiment Tried," *Independent* 26 (Mar. 5, 1874).

16. "Miss Phelps Lectures," *Boston University Beacon* 2 (Nov. 15, 1876): 28-29, available in the Special Collections, Boston Archives, Mugar Library, Boston University; letter Phelps [Ward] to George Eliot, Dec. 1, 1876, Beinicke Rare Book and Manuscript Library, Yale University; *Chapters*, pp. 254-55.

17. "A Woman's Professorship in Boston University," *Woman's Journal* 9 (Mar. 30, 1878):101; see also Archives of the Massachusetts Society for the University Education of Women (MSUEW), Mugar Library, Boston University, a society of which both Claflin and Phelps were members.

18. Edward H. Clarke, *Sex in Education* (Boston: J. R. Osgood, 1873); Chapter 7 of *Sex in Education*, Julia Ward Howe, ed.

19. *The Trotty Book* and *Trotty's Wedding Tour, and Storybook* (Boston, 1870 and 1873 respectively); on "Sensible Girls," see letter to Benjamin H. Ticknor, Oct. 4, 1872, Houghton Library, Harvard University; on "Lily," see Bennett, *Phelps*, pp. 37-38, and *Austin Phelps: A Memoir* pp. 121-23.

20. Bennett, *Phelps*, pp. 41, 149; *My Cousin and I* (London, 1879); "Our Little Woman" and "Hannah Colby's Chance," *Our Young Folks* 8 (Nov.-Dec., 1872) and 9 (Oct.-Dec., 1873) respectively; "Our Little Woman," *Woman's Journal* 4 (Feb. 2-22, 1873). Page references to *Our Young Folks* serializations are cited in the text.

21. "What They Are Doing," *Independent* 23 (Aug. 17, 1871).

22. "A Brave Girl," *Wide Awake* 18-19. Ensuing references in the text are to volume and page number.

23. John Greenleaf Whittier, Dec. 27, [1883] Friends Historical Library, Swarthmore College.

24. See Nina Baym, *Woman's Fiction: A Guide to Novels by and about Women in America, 1820–1870* (Ithaca: Cornell University Press, 1978), pp. 296-98, for a discussion of this pattern.

25. Phelps to G. Eliot, Dec. 1, 1876, Beinecke Rare Book and Manuscript Library, Yale University; see *Chapters,* pp. 192-229, 242, for her life in Gloucester.

26. Phelps to Mary Claflin, Saturday [1876-187?], Rutherford B. Hayes Library, Fremont, Ohio; to J. R. Osgood, June 28, 1877, Historical Society of Pennsylvania; from H. W. Longfellow, July 19, 1877, Boston Public Library; to H. W. Longfellow, July 18, and Aug. 18, [?1879], Houghton Library, Harvard University; to Mr. and Mrs. [Edwin Percy] Whipple, Aug. 27, [?1881], Beinecke Rare Book and Manuscript Library, Yale University; *Chapters*, pp. 219-20 on Phillips Brooks, pp. 166-68 on Oliver Wendell Holmes.

27. Phelps to W. H. Ward, Nov. 7, 1875; "Going South" and "Confessions of St. Augustine," *Atlantic Monthly* 37 (Jan. & Feb., 1876):25-34 and 129-40.

28. "A Florida Engraving" and "A Florida Water-Color," *Independent* 27 (Dec. 30, 1875) and 28 (Jan. 6, 1876):1-2 and 1-2.

29. *An Old Maid's Paradise* (Boston, 1879) and *Independent* 31 (June-Sept., 1879); *Burglars in Paradise* (Boston, 1886) and *Independent* 38 (Feb.-Apr., 1886). Both were reissued in the Riverside Paper Series, *Old Maid* as #9 (1885) and *Burglars* as #14 (1886), and again in a one-volume edition as *Old Maids and Burglars in Paradise* (Boston, 1887, 1898); references in the text are to the 1898 reissue. Parts of the following discussion previously appeared in my "The Feminist Mock-Heroics of Elizabeth Stuart Phelps (1844–1911)," *Regionalism and the Female Imagination* 3 (Fall/Winter, 1977):20-28.

30. *The Burglar Who Moved Paradise* (Boston: Houghton, Mifflin, 1897), allegedly written by Phelps's husband, Herbert Dickinson Ward, but showing her style and tone after the first chapter, offered an affirmative response to this inquiry. Of interest is the fact that although the description in the book tells us the husband looks after Corona, the action reveals that she looks after him, a pattern of female-male relations that the earlier *Paradise* books had set.

31. "Elizabeth S. Phelps and Dr. Mary [Briggs] Harris," unsigned and undated typescript in "Phelps House" folder, Andover Historical Society, Andover, Massachusetts.

32. Phelps to W. D. Howells, Mar. 10, 1880, Houghton Library, Harvard University. *Friends: A Duet* (Boston, 1881) and *Atlantic Monthly* 47 (Jan.-Aug., 1881); page references to the book appear in the text.

33. "A Dream within a Dream," *Independent* 26 (Feb. 19, 1874).

34. *Doctor Zay* (Boston, 1882) and *Atlantic Monthly* 49-50 (Apr.-Sept., 1882); page references in the text refer to the book.

35. Phelps to Howells, Nov. 2, 1881, Houghton Library, Harvard University; "Phelps-Harris" typescript, Andover Historical Society.

36. Phelps to Howells, Nov. 2, 1881, Houghton Library, Harvard University. A[lice] S[tone] B[lackwell], review of *Dr. Breen's Practice* by W. D. Howells, *Woman's Journal* 12 (Dec. 3, 1881):389; A[lice] S[tone] B[lackwell], review of *A Country Doctor* by S. O. Jewett, *Woman's Journal* 15 (June 1, 1884):199.

37. See Bibliography for listing of stories appearing in Collections. Bennett, cited as secondary source, lists all uncollected stories.

38. Austin Phelps, *My Portfolio: A Collection of Essays* (New York, 1882), pp. 94-104; *Woman's Journal* 9 (Aug. 12, 1878):270, and editor-

ial rebuttal, 268; L. Stone (p. 273) and H. B. Blackwell (p. 276), also rebutted; comparable responses followed in September issues.

39. A Phelps, *Portfolio*, pp. 105-16; see "Unhappy Girls," *Independent* 23 (1871), and Phelps to G. Eliot, Feb. 26, 1873, Beinecke Rare Book and Manuscript Library, Yale University.

40. L. Clark Seelye, *The Early History of Smith College, 1871-1910* (Boston: Houghton, Mifflin, 1923), pp. 45, 61; *Beyond the Gates* (Boston, 1883), p. 4; "Elizabeth Stuart Phelps," [Boston] *Sunday Herald*, rpt. *Woman's Journal* 11 (June 12, 1880):190; Phelps [Ward], *A. Phelps*, pp. 141-44.

41. Phelps to John Greenleaf Whittier, Sept. 3, 1884, Houghton Library, Harvard University.

Chapter Four

1. *Chapters*, p. 157, 273.

2. Phelps to Harriet Prescott Spofford, Feb. 2, 1903, Miscellaneous Manuscripts, American Antiquarian Society, Worcester, Massachusetts.

3. *McClure's Magazine* 6 (Dec. 1895–Nov., 1896):362; see her mother's *A Peep at "Number Five"; or, A Chapter in the Life of a City Pastor*, H. Trusta, pseud. (Boston, 1852), a novel revealing the life of a pastor's wife.

4. Lilian Whiting, *Boston Days* (Boston: Little Brown, 1902), p. 432.

5. Phelps to Jewett, Dec. 16, [1879], Houghton Library, Harvard University.

6. Phelps to Spofford, 1903.

7. See *Chapters*, chaps. 7-9, 11; Carol Farley Kessler, "'The Woman's Hour,'" chap. 5A, cites sources. See also tributes to friends in verse, in *Songs of the Silent World and Other Poems* (Boston, 1885).

8. "The Empty Column," *Independent* 36 (Sept. 4, 1884).

9. Phelps to William Hayes Ward, Nov. 1, 1885, James Duncan Phillips Library, Essex Institute, Salem, Massachusetts. For further discussion of the marriage, see Bennett, *Phelps*, chap. 8.

10. *Dictionary of American Biography* (1936), s. v. "Ward, Herbert Dickinson," by G[eorge] F. W[hicher]; Mary B. Claflin, *Under the Old Elms* (New York: Crowell, 1895), p. 92.

11. Phelps to W. H. Ward, Aug. 22, 1884, [Oct. 1885], Nov. 1, 1885, Phillips Library, Essex Institute.

12. Phelps to Whittier, Dec. 17, [1885], Essex Institute; Whittier to Phelps, Dec. 20, 1885, Friends Historical Library, Swarthmore College.

13. Whittier to Phelps, Apr. 8 and 17, 1886, Swarthmore; Phelps to Richard Watson Gilder, Mar. 6, 1887, Century Collection, New York Public Library; Whittier to Phelps, Apr. 11 and May 14, 18, 26, 1888, Swarthmore; Phelps to W. H. Ward, May 15, 1888, Clifton Waller Barrett Collection, Alderman Library, University of Virginia.

14. Phelps to Hetta Ward, [late spring], July 28 and 30, 1888, Essex Institute.

15. Phelps to Whittier, Oct. 23, 1888, Essex Institute.

16. Phelps to John Greenleaf Whittier, Jan. 20 1889, Essex Institute. Bennett, *Phelps*, p. 91, misinterprets Phelps's facetiousness in this letter. I believe Phelps jokes unsentimentally about married life.

17. Phelps to Spofford, 1903.

18. All of the published fiction for adults by "H. Trusta" [pseud.] has been microfilmed as part of the collection *American Fiction, 1774-1900*, Lyle H. Wright, ed. (New Haven: Research Publications, 1974): *The Sunny Side; or, The Country Minister's Wife* (Boston, 1851); *The Angel over the Right Shoulder* (Andover, 1852); and *The Tell-Tale: or Home Secrets Told by Old Travellers* (Boston, 1853), pp. 96-134. See also Kessler, "A Literary Legacy: Elizabeth Stuart Phelps, Mother and Daughter," *Frontiers: A Journal of Women Studies* 5 no. 3 (Fall 1980):28-33.

19. Phelps to Henry Wadsworth Longfellow, Mar. 21, 1879, Houghton Library, Harvard University; to John Greenleaf Whittier, May 2, 1881, Alderman Library, University of Virginia; to George Eliot, May 27, 1877, Beinecke Rare Book and Manuscript Library, Yale University.

20. Phelps to George Eliot, Feb. 26, 1873, Beinecke Rare Book and Manuscript Library, Yale University.

21. Tillie Olsen, *Silences* (New York: Delta, 1978), pp. 9, 10, 17.

22. See T[homas] W[entworth] Higginson, "Late Books by American Women," *Woman's Journal* 2 (Dec. 9, 1871):385; M. L. C., "Gail Hamilton's Criticism," *Woman's Journal* 9 (Mar. 30, 1878):99.

23. For Alcott, see Madeleine Stern, ed., *Behind the Mask* and *Plots and Counterplots* (New York: Morrow, 1975 and 1976, respectively).

24. Mary Roberts Coolidge, *Why Women Are So* (1912; rpt. New York: Arno, 1972), pp. 285-86.

25. *Austin Phelps: A Memoir* (New York, 1891), p. 87.

26. *The Story of Avis* (Boston, 1877); hereafter page references cited in the text.

27. Harriet Prescott Spofford, "The Amber Gods," *Atlantic Monthly* 4 (Jan.-Feb., 1860):7-18, 170-85; in *American Voices, American Women,* eds. L. R. Edwards and A. Diamond (New York: Avon, 1973). See Phelps, "Stories That Stay," *Century* 59 (Nov., 1910).

28. Quoted by Phelps from George Eliot, "Armgart," a verse drama first appearing in *Macmillan's Magazine* and *Atlantic Monthly* (July, 1870).

29. Phelps to James R. Osgood, Feb. 7, 1877, Barnard College Library. Phelps used the Sphinx in two poems (*Songs of the Silent World,* Boston, 1884, pp. 97-99) in the context of eliciting an answer to the riddle of womanhood.

30. Helen Waite Papashvily, *All the Happy Endings* (New York: Harper, 1956), chap. 6, "The Death of the Master," pp. 63-74.

31. L[ucy] S[tone], review of *The Story of Avis* in "Literary Notices," *Woman's Journal* 8 (Dec. 15, 1877) :400; "A Dream within a Dream," *Independent* 26 (Feb. 19, 1874).

32. Phelps to Henry Wadsworth Longfellow, Mar. 21, 1879, Houghton Library, Harvard University.

33. Phelps to William Dean Howells, Mar. 10, 1880, Houghton Library, Harvard University.

34. *The Madonna of the Tubs* (Boston, 1886); also in *Harper's New Monthly Magazine* 72 (Dec., 1885), and *Fourteen to One* (Boston, 1891). References are to the 1886 book.

35. *Donald Marcy* (Boston, 1893); Phelps to Spofford, 1903.

36. Phelps to Henry Oscar Houghton, Apr. 14, 1894, Houghton Library, Harvard University; *A Singular Life* (Boston 1895), and *Atlantic Monthly* 75 (Jan.-Oct., 1895)—references are to the book; Alice P. Hackett, *Fifty Years of Best Sellers, 1895-1945* (New York: Bowker, 1945), p. 12.

37. *Jack, The Fisherman* (Boston, 1887); also as "Jack," *Century* 12 (June, 1887) and in *Fourteen to One* (Boston, 1891). References are to the 1887 book.

38. Phelps to Richard Watson Gilder, June 22, 1887, Century Collection, New York Public Library.

39. See Phelps's discussion of Mary Magdalene in *The Story of Jesus Christ: An Interpretation* (Boston, 1897), esp. pp. 200-201.

40. Elizabeth Cady Stanton, ed., *The Woman's Bible* (1895, 1898; rpt. Seattle: Coalition Task Force, 1974).

41. Nancy Sahli, "Smashing: Women's Relationships before the Fall," *Chrysalis,* no. 8 (Summer, 1979), pp. 17-28.

42. On women's issues, see *Woman's Journal* masthead from 15 (Feb., 1884) to 42 (Jan., 1911); "Andover Woman Suffrage League," *Woman's Journal* 18 (May 7, 1887) :148. On reading room, see "Concerning Women," *Woman's Journal* 20 (Aug. 10, 1889). On dress, see "Concerning Women," *Woman's Journal* 21 (Sept. 13, 1890); "The Décolleté in Modern Life," *Forum* 9 (Aug., 1890).

43. "Miss Phelps and Howells," *Woman's Journal* 18 (Oct. 8, 1887):322.

Chapter Five

1. Phelps Ward to Elizabeth Garver Jordan, July 10, 1905, New York Public Library.

2. Sahli, "Smashing."

3. *The Successors of Mary the First* (Boston, 1901) and *Ladies' Home Journal* 17 (Oct. 1900-Apr. 1901). References in the text are to the book.

4. "The World Invisible," Part III, *Harper's Bazar* 42 (July, 1908):620.

5. *Avery* (Boston, 1902); also published as "His Wife," *Harper's New Monthly Magazine* 103 (Sept.-Nov., 1901). References in the text are to the book.

6. Hans Toch, *The Social Psychology of Social Movements* (New York: Bobbs-Merrill, 1965), p. 44.

7. Mary Adams [pseud.], *Confessions of a Wife* (New York, 1902) and *Century Magazine* 41 (Apr.-Nov., 1902)—references in the text are

to the book; "Concerning Women," *Woman's Journal* 33 (July 12, 1902).

8. *Chapters,* pp. 64, 237-39; see the advertisement in *Woman's Journal* 24 (Dec. 16, 1893) :399.

9. *Trixy* (Boston, 1904); *Loveliness* (Boston, 1899).

10. "Address," Mar. 16, 1903, p. 8, located in the Rutherford B. Hayes Library, Fremont, Ohio; their Claflin Papers also contain some of her correspondence on the subject.

11. *The Man in the Case* (Boston, 1906) and *Ladies' Home Journal* 23 (Feb.-July, 1906); references in the text are to the book.

12. *Walled In: A Novel* (Boston, 1907) and *Harper's Bazar* 40-41 (Dec. 1906-Dec. 1907); references in the text are to the book.

13. For writing women, Papashvily, *All the Happy Endings,* chaps. 6 "The Death of the Master" and 7 "The Mutilation of the Male," pp. 63-94.

14. *Though Life Us Do Part* (Boston, 1908) and *Woman's Home Companion* 34 (Nov. 1907-July, 1908). References in the text are to the book.

15. Phelps expressed a similar view in a letter to the managing editor of the *Boston Herald,* Jan. 18, 1892 (Alderman Library, University of Virginia): she apparently enclosed a clipping of her article "There Should Be No War."

16. Horney, *Neurosis and Human Growth,* pp. 155-75.

17. On writing for income, see Phelps Ward to A. A. Fields, Oct. 18, 1889, Houghton Library, Harvard University; to M. B. D. Claflin, Good Friday, 1893, Rutherford B. Hayes Library, Fremont, Ohio; to E. Bok, Jan. 8 and Dec. 31, 1904, Alderman Library, University of Virginia.

18. *The Whole Family: A Novel By Twelve Authors* (New York, 1908). Phelps, Chap. 8, "The Married Daughter," appeared in *Harper's Bazar* 42 (July, 1908). See letters to Jordan, Feb. 18, 23 and Mar. 18, 1907, Elizabeth Jordan Papers, Manuscripts and Archives Division, Astor, Lenox and Tilden Foundations, New York Public Library.

19. Letter to Jordan, Apr. 11, 1900, Elizabeth Jordan Papers, New York Public Library; *The Oath of Allegiance* (Boston, 1909) and *The Empty House* (Boston, 1910); *Jonathan and David* (New York, 1909).

20. *Comrades* (New York, 1911) and *Harper's New Monthly Magazine* 123 (August, 1911). References in the text are to the book.

21. Phelps Ward from Henry Mills Alden, Sept. 22, 1905, American Antiquarian Society, Worcester, Massachusetts; "The Windsor Club Stories," *Independent* 72 (Feb. 1, 1912); Bennett, *Phelps,* pp. 134-35.

22. *Dictionary of American Biography* (1936), s. v. "Ward," by W[hicher]; letter to E. G. Jordan, Feb. 18, 1907, New York Public Library.

23. Phelps Ward, Feb. 2, 1903, Miscellaneous Manuscripts, American Antiquarian Society.

Chapter Six

1. On the business of authorship, see Susan Coultrap-McQuin, "Elizabeth Stuart Phelps: The Cultural Context of a Nineteenth-Century Professional Writer," Ph. D. dissertation, Universtity of Iowa, 1979; "Editorial and Publishing Relationships," pp. 168-212. On personal problems regarding authorship, see Phelps [Ward], *Chapters,* pp. 80-81, 266-68. For her estate, see Will #87702, 2nd series, Elizabeth Stuart Phelps Ward, Newton, at Probate Court, Middlesex County Courthouse, Cambridge, Massachusetts. On why her verse sold, see letter to William Hayes Ward, Sept. 21, 1876, Essex Institute.

2. *Within the Gates* (Boston, 1901); "The Veteran," *Pocket Magazine* (New York) 1 (Nov., 1895) :59-84. *Poetic Studies* (Boston, 1875) and *Songs of the Silent World and Other Poems* (Boston, 1884); see letters from Whittier, June 6, 1875 and Nov. 1886, Friends Historical Library, Swarthmore, and from Longfellow, May 16, 1879, Boston Public Library. For a discussion of the verse, see Bennett, *Phelps,* chap. 9 "Verse," and Bibliography, pp. 154-58; "Conemaugh," *Independent* 51 (June 27, 1889) :817; "The Stone Woman of Eastern Point," *Harper's New Monthly Magazine* 84 (Feb., 1892) :436-37.

3. For addresses, see "A Plea for the Helpless," [New York]: American Humane Association, [Mar. 11, 1901]; "Vivisection and Legislation in Massachusetts," Philadelphia: American Anti-Vivisection Society, [Mar., 14 1902]; Address before Committee on Probate and Chancery on the bill "Further to Prevent Cruelty to Animals in Massachusetts," [n. p., Mar. 16, 1903], Rutherford B. Hayes Library, Fremont, Ohio. See Bibliography in Bennett, pp. 142, 150-54, for full anti-vivisection listing and for nonfiction in serials. For memorials, see "In Memoriam: James T. Fields," *Independent* 33 (June 2, 1881):1-2; "In

Memoriam: Edward Rowland Sill," *Independent* 39 (Apr. 28, 1887): 517-18 and "Edward Rowland Sill," *Century* 14 (Sept., 1888):704-8; "Whittier," *Century* 45 (Jan., 1893):363-68; "Phillips Brooks: The Last Time," *Independent* 45 (Feb. 16, 1893):205-6; "The Bearer Falls" (Lucy Larcom), *Independent* 45 (May 4, 1893):603-4; "Heaven: The Gates Ajar—25 Years After," *North American Review,* May, 1893; *A Gracious Life* (Boston: no imprint, 1888).

4. "The World Invisible," Part II, *Harper's Bazar* 52 (May, 1908):421.

5. On McClure, see William Webster Ellsworth, *A Golden Age of Authors* (Boston: Houghton, Mifflin, 1919), p. 130; *The Story of Jesus Christ* (Boston, 1897), p. viii, 200-201.

6. Phelps [Ward] and Ward, *A Lost Hero* (Boston, 1891); on children's literature, see R. Gordon Kelly, *Mother Was a Lady: Self and Society in Selected American Children's Periodicals, 1865-1890* (Westport, Conn.: Greenwood Press, 1974), pp. 32-55.

7. For a complete listing of uncollected fiction, see Bibliography in Bennett, pp. 143-50. Gift editions included *The Madonna of the Tubs,* 1886; *Jack the Fisherman,* 1887; *The Supply at St. Agatha's,* 1896; and *Loveliness: A Story,* 1899, all Houghton, Mifflin; *Jonathan and David,* 1909; *A Chariot of Fire,* 1910; *Comrades,* 1911, from Harper. All short story collections were published by Houghton, Mifflin.

8. Letters from O. W. Holmes, Oct. 29, 1879, Boston Public Library, and from Whittier, Dec. 12, 1879, Swarthmore College; review of *Sealed Orders* in "Current Fiction," *Literary World* 10 (Oct. 25, 1879):341.

9. On "Madonna," letter from Whittier, Dec. 4, 1885, Swarthmore, and *Saturday Review* 63 (Mar. 26, 1887):451; on "Jack," letter from Holmes, May 4, 1888, Boston Public Library, and *Nation* 45 (Dec. 15, 1887):485; on *Fourteen to One, Atlantic* 68 (Nov., 1891):710-11.

10. *Saturday Review* 109 (Jan. 29, 1910):144 and *Nation* 89 (Nov. 18, 1909):487-88.

11. "Zerviah Hope," *Scribner's Magazine* 21 (Nov., 1880):78-88; letter from Whittier, Nov. 24, 1880, Swarthmore.

12. Obituary notices cited include "Mrs. E. S. P. Ward Dies in 67th Year," *New York Times,* Jan. 29, 1911, p. 11, col. 1; "Elizabeth Stuart Phelps Ward," *Independent* 70 (Feb. 2, 1911):269; *Woman's Journal* 42 (Feb. 4, 1911):40; Ella Gilbert Ives, "Elizabeth Stuart P. Ward: A More Intimate Sketch of Her Personality," *Boston Transcript* (Feb. 4, 1911).

13. London: *Athenaeum* 2266 (Apr. 1, 1871):399; *Saturday Review of Politics, Literature, Science, and Art* 31 (May 6, 1871):573-74; United

States: *Literary World* 1 (Apr. 1, 1871):165–67; *Harper's New Monthly Magazine* 43 (June, 1871):300–1.

14. For reviews, see *Harper's* 56 (Jan., 1878):310; *Literary World* 8 (Nov. 1, 1877):97–98; *Nation* 26 (Mar. 21, 1878):202; *Woman's Journal* 8 (Dec. 15, 1877):400 and 9 (Mar. 30, 1878):99. See letters from Longfellow, Oct. 30, 1877, Boston Public Library; from Whittier, Nov. 17, 1877, Friends Historical Library, Swarthmore College; from S. K. Bolton, Apr. 5, 1878, American Antiquarian Society, Worcester, Massachusetts.

15. For reviews, see *Critic* 2 (Dec. 2, 1882):325–26; *Independent* 34 (Nov. 16, 1882):10; *Literary World* 13 (Nov. 4, 1882):371; *Woman's Journal* 13 (Sept. 2, 1882):278. See letters from Whittier, Oct. 21, 1882, Friends Historical Library, Swarthmore College; from Larcom, Oct. 22, 1882, Radcliffe College.

16. For reviews, see *Dial* 20 (Feb. 1, 1896):80; *Independent* 47 (Dec. 12, 1895):1690; *Literary World* 26 (Nov. 16, 1895):388; *Woman's Journal* 26 (Oct. 19, 1895):331. Monroe Stevens, "The *A Singular Life* Reviewed and Gloucester Vindicated," [Gloucester], 1896.

17. T. W. Higginson, *Woman's Journal* 2 (Dec. 9, 1871):49. Letter from E. R. Sill, Jan. 1, 1884, Wellesley College. "Sojourner," "Miss Phelps and Howells," *Woman's Journal* 18 (Oct. 8, 1887):322. Willa Cather quoted in *Women & Literature* 3 (1975):11. Letter to J. R. Osgood, Apr. 26, 1871, Houghton Library, Harvard University. *Montgomery Ward and Co. Catalogue and Buyers' Guide* (1895; rpt. New York: Dover, 1969), p. 57; Karl Baedeker, *United States* (1893; rpt. New York: DaCapo, 1971), pp. 92, 94.

18. Fred Lewis Pattee, *History of American Literature* (New York: Century, 1915), pp. 221–24.

19. V. L. Parrington, *Main Currents in American Thought* (New York: Harcourt, 1930), 3:60–69.

20. Arthur Hobson Quinn, *American Fiction* (New York: Appleton-Century-Crofts, 1936), pp. 192–204,

21. Van Wyck Brooks, *New England: Indian Summer* (New York: E. P. Dutton, 1940), pp. 82, 99, 155–56.

22. Bennett, Bibliography, pp. 139–59; Margaret Wyman [Langworthy], "Women in the American Realistic Novel, 1860–1893: Literary Reflection of Social Fact," Ph. D. dissertation, Radcliffe College, 1950, pp. 243–72. Also of the period, a discussion adding no additional viewpoint appears in Perry D. Westbrook, *Acres of Flint: Writers of*

Rural New England, 1870-1900 (Washington, D. C.: Scarecrow Press, 1951), pp. 13-16.

23. James D. Hart, *The Popular Book* (New York: Oxford, 1950), chap. 7, pp. 106-24.

24. Smith, Introduction, *The Gates Ajar,* pp. v-xxxiii.

25. Welter, *Dimity Convictions,* pp. 111-20; St. Armand, *American Quarterly* 29 (1977):55-78; Douglas, *The Feminization of American Culture* (1977), pp. 223-26.

26. Stansell, *Massachusetts Review* 13 (1972):239-56; Douglas Wood, *Journal of Interdisciplinary History* 4 (1973):51-52; Habegger, *PMLA* 91 (1976):891-92.

27. Edwards and Diamond, *American Voices, American Women,* pp. 13-15; Stewart, *Women's Studies* 6 (1979):133-35, and also in *A New Mythos,* pp. 110-11.

28. Kessler, Ph. D. dissertation, University of Pennsylvania, 1977; Coultrap-McQuin, Ph. D. dissertation, University of Iowa, 1979; Kelly, Ph. D. dissertation, University of North Carolina, 1979.

29. Florence Howe, "Those We Still Don't Read," *College English* 43 (Jan., 1981):14. For Phelps's work in print, see bibliography.

30. *Austin Phelps: A Memoir* (1891), p. 87, written by Phelps of her mother.

31. Whittier to T. Franklin Currier, Mar. 5, 1877, in *The Letters of John Greenleaf Whittier,* Vol. 3, John B. Pickard, ed. (Cambridge: Belknap Press, Harvard University Press, 1975), pp. 186-87, n. 3.

Selected Bibliography

PRIMARY SOURCES

1. Book-length fiction

Avery. Boston and New York: Houghton, Mifflin, 1902. Also "His Wife," *Harper's New Monthly* 103 (Sept.-Nov., 1901):518-28, 701-11, 895-905.

Beyond the Gates. Boston and New York: Houghton, Mifflin, 1883.

Burglars in Paradise. Boston and New York: Houghton, Mifflin, 1886. Also *Independent* 38 (Feb.-Apr., 1886):129-30, 161-62, 194-95, 250-51, 286-87, 318-19, 350-51, 382-83, 414-15, 446-47, 478-79, 509-10.

Confessions of a Wife (pseud. Mary Adams). New York: Century, 1902. Also *Century* (Apr.-Nov., 1902):41:945-56; 42:135-48, 266-77, 453-64, 558-71, 732-45, 884-93; 43:26-39.

Doctor Zay. Boston and New York: Houghton, Mifflin, 1882. Also *Atlantic Monthly* (Apr.-Sept., 1882) 49:518-30, 630-50, 764-79; 50:28-41, 206-13, 325-39.

Friends: A Duet. Boston: Houghton, Mifflin, 1881. Also *Atlantic Monthly* (Jan.-Aug., 1881), 47:86-95, 145-55, 305-17, 490-507, 666-78, 836-44; 48:98-106.

The Gates Ajar. Boston: Fields, Osgood, 1868.

The Gates Between. Boston and New York: Houghton, Mifflin, 1887.

Hedged In. Boston: Fields, Osgood, 1870.

"Jane Gurley's Story." *Hours at Home* (Mar.-Oct., 1866), 2:406-12, 494-502; 3:19-30, 168-74, 250-59, 239-47, 421-26, 538-45.

The Man in the Case. Boston and New York: Houghton, Mifflin, 1906. Also *Ladies' Home Journal* 23(1906):5-6, 48(Feb.); 13-14(Apr.); 13-14(May); 13-14, 48 (July).

An Old Maid's Paradise. Boston: Houghton, Osgood, 1879. Also *Independent* 31 (1879); 1 (June 26); 3-4 (July 3); 1-3 (July 17); 1-2

(July 24); 2-3 (July 31); 3 (Aug. 7); 1-2 (Aug. 14); 2-3 (Aug. 21); 3-4 (Aug. 28); 3 (Sept. 4); 2-3 (Sept. 11); 2-3 (Sept. 18).

The Silent Partner. Boston: James R. Osgood, 1871. Reprinted in Americans in Fiction Series, Clarence Gohdes, ed. Ridgewood, New Jersey: Gregg Press, 1967, distributed by Irvington Publishers, New York; with afterword by Mari Jo Buhle and Florence Howe, Old Westbury, NY: Feminist Press, 1982.

A Singular Life. Boston and New York: Houghton, Mifflin, 1895. Also *Atlantic Monthly* (Jan.-Oct., 1895), 75:1-36, 145-64, 353-69, 433-45, 641-53, 721-36; 76:77-90, 145-61, 380-97, 433-48.

The Story of Avis. Boston: James R. Osgood, 1877. Reprinted in Rediscovered Fiction by American Women, Elizabeth Hardwick, ed., New York: Arno, 1977. Excerpted *American Voices, American Women,* Lee R. Edwards and Arlyn Diamond, eds., New York: Avon, 1973, pp. 65-150.

The Successors of Mary the First. Boston and New York: Houghton, Mifflin, 1901. Also *Ladies' Home Journal,* 17 (Oct., 1900-Apr., 1901), 5-6, 15-16, 13-14, 9-10, 9-10, 13-14, 13-14.

Though Life Us Do Part. Boston and New York: Houghton, Mifflin, 1908. Also *Woman's Home Companion* (Dec., 1907-July, 1908), 34:6-8, 70; 19-20, 68-69; 35:19-21, 54; 15-16, 44-46, 17-18, 58; 17-18, 54; 15-16, 49-50; 19-20, 52-53; 19-20, 47.

Trixy. Boston and New York: Houghton, Mifflin, 1904.

Walled In: A Novel. Boston and New York: Houghton, Mifflin, 1907. Also *Harper's Bazar* (Dec., 1906-Dec., 1907), 40, 1107-19; 41, 40-47, 125-30, 233-41, 373-80, 440-45, 560-67, 656-64, 739-46, 839-47, 979-88, 1043-49, 1177-88.

The Whole Family: A Novel by Twelve Authors. New York: Harper, 1908. Chap. 8: "The Married Daughter," pp. 185-218. Also *Harper's Bazar* 42 (July, 1908):636-47.

2. Juvenile fiction

"A Brave Girl," *Wide Awake* (Dec., 1883-Aug., 1884), 18:27-31, 105-111, 169, 174, 237-241, 297-303, 361-65; 19:27-31, 92-96, 156-62.

Donald Marcy. Boston and New York: Houghton, Mifflin, 1893.

"Gypsy" series: Graves and Young, Boston. *Gypsy Breynton, Gypsy's Cousin Joy, Gypsy's Sowing and Reaping,* 1865. *Gypsy's Year at the Golden Crescent,* 1866.

Mercy Gliddon's Work. Boston: Henry Hoyt, 1865.

My Cousin and I. London: Sunday School Union, 1879. Also *Our Young Folks:* "Our Little Woman," 8 (Nov.-Dec., 1872), 654-62, 727-37; "Hannah Colby's Chance," 9 (Oct.-Dec., 1873), 595-604, 653-60, 730-40; *The Woman's Journal* 4 (Feb. 8, 15, 22, 1873).

"Tiny" series: Massachusetts Sabbath Day School Society, Boston. *Ellen's Idol,* 1864. *Tiny,* 1866. *Tiny's Sunday Nights; I Don't Know How,* 1867.

"Trotty" series: *The Trotty Book.* Boston: Fields, Osgood, 1870. *Trotty's Wedding Tour, and Story-book.* Boston: J. R. Osgood, 1873.

Up Hill; or, Life in the Factory. Boston: Henry Hoyt, 1865.

3. Essays

"The Décolleté in Modern Life." *Forum* 9 (Aug., 1890):670-84.

"A Dream within a Dream." *Independent* 26 (Feb. 19, 1874):1.

"The Empty Column" [Mary Clemmer Ames]. *Independent* 36 (Sept. 4, 1884):1121-22.

"The Experiment Tried." *Independent* 26 (Mar. 5, 1874):1-2.

"The 'Female Education' of Women." *Independent* 25 (Nov. 13, 1873):1409-10, and *Woman's Journal* 4 (Nov. 22, 1873):371.

"A Few Words to the Girls." *Woman's Journal* 3 (Feb. 24, 1872):62.

"George Eliot." *Harper's Weekly* 29 (Feb. 14, 1885):102-3.

"George Eliot's Short Stories." *Independent* 37 (Apr. 30, 1885):545-46.

"The Gist of the Matter." *Independent* 23 (July 13, 1871):1, and *Woman's Journal* 2 (July 22, 1871):29.

"Heaven: The Gates Ajar—25 Years After." *North American Review* 156 (May, 1893):567-76.

"The Higher Claim." *Independent* 23 (Oct. 5, 1871):1, and *Woman's Journal* 2 (Oct. 28, 1871):43.

"Last Words from George Eliot." *Harper's New Monthly* 64 (Mar., 1882):568-71.

"Men and Muscle." *Independent* 23 (Aug. 31, 1871):1.

"The New Earth." *Independent* 23 (Sept. 28, 1871):1.

"Rights and Relatives." *Independent* 23 (Sept. 7, 1871):3, and *Woman's Journal* 2 (Sept. 23, 1871):38.

"Song of the Shirt." *Independent* 23 (Aug. 10, 1871):1, and *Woman's Journal* 2 (Sept. 2, 1871):35.

"Stories That Stay." *Century* 58 (Nov. 1910):118-23.

"Supporting Herself." *St. Nicholas* 11 (May, 1884):517-19.

"A Talk to Girls." *Independent* 24 (Jan. 4, 1872):1, and *Woman's Journal* 3 (Jan. 27, 1872):30.

"Too Much Conscience." *Independent* 23 (Aug. 3, 1871):3, and *Woman's Journal* 2 (Aug. 19, 1871):33.

"'The True Woman.'" *Independent* 23 (Oct. 19, 1871):1.

"Unhappy Girls." *Independent* 23 (July 27, 1871):1, and *Woman's Journal* 2 (Aug. 12, 1871):32.

"'The United Head.'" *Independent* 23 (Sept. 14, 1871):1, and *Woman's Journal* 2 (Sept. 30, 1871):39.

"What Shall They Do?" *Harper's New Monthly* 35 (Sept., 1867):519-23.

"What They Are Doing." *Independent* 23 (Aug. 17, 1871):1.

"Where It Goes." *Independent* 23 (July 20, 1871):1

"Why Shall They Do It?." *Harper's New Monthly* 36 (Jan., 1868):218-23..

"Women and Money." *Independent* 23 (Aug. 24, 1871):1.

"The World Invisible." Pts. 1-3, *Harper's Bazar* 52 (April-May, July, 1908):354-56, 419-22, 619-23.

4. Miscellaneous prose works

Austin Phelps: A Memoir. New York: Charles Scribner's, 1891.

Chapters from a Life. Boston and New York: Houghton, Mifflin, 1896. Also *McClure's* (Dec. 1895-Nov. 1896), 6:49-58, 191-98, 293-300, 361-68, 490-95, 513-18; 7:3-11, 114-21, 234-44, 353-62, 461-68; 8:77-85. Reprinted in Signal Lives Series, Annette Baxter, ed., New York: Arno, 1980.

In *Sex and Education: A Reply to Dr. E. H. Clarke's "Sex in Education."* Edited by Julia Ward Howe. Chapter 7 (pp. 126-38) by Elizabeth Stuart Phelps. Boston: Roberts Bros., 1874.

The Story of Jesus Christ: An Interpretation. Boston and New York: Houghton, Mifflin, 1897.

The Struggle for Immortality. Boston and New York: Houghton, Mifflin, 1889. Contains "What Is a Fact?" "Is God Good?" "What Does Revelation Reveal?" "The Struggle for Immortality," "The Christianity of Christ," "The [Great] Psychical Opportunity," "The Psychical Wave."

What to Wear? Boston: J. R. Osgood, 1873. Also "Women's Dress," *Independent* 25 (May 1-22, 1873):547-48, 579, 611 642.

5. Short fiction

The Empty House and Other Stories. Boston and New York: Houghton, Mifflin, 1910. Contains "The Empty House," "Twenty-four: Four," "The Presence," "The Romance of the Bill," "Fée," "His Father's Heart," "The Rejected Manuscript," "Sweet Home Road," "The Joy-Giver."

Fourteen to One. Boston and New York: Houghton, Mifflin, 1891. Contains "Fourteen to One," "The Bell of St. Basil's," "Shut In," "Jack the Fisherman," "The Madonna of the Tubs," "A Brave Deed," "The Sacrifice of Antigone," "Sweet Home," "Too Late," "The Reverend Malachi Matthew," "His Relict," "Mary Elizabeth," "Annie Laurie," "The Law and the Gospel."

Men, Women, and Ghosts. Boston: Fields, Osgood, 1879. Contains "No News," "The Tenth of January," "Night-Watches" ("Voices of the Night"), "The Day of My Death," " 'Little Tommy Tucker,' " "One of the Elect" ("Magdalene"), "What Was the Matter?" "In the Gray Goth," "Calico," "Kentucky's Ghost."

The Oath of Allegiance and Other Stories. Boston and New York: Houghton, Mifflin, 1909. Contains "The Oath of Allegiance," "Covered Embers," "The Autobiography of Aureola," "A Chariot of Fire," "His Soul to Keep," "A Sacrament," " 'Tammyshanty,' " "Unemployed," "The Sacred Fire," "Christophorus," "The Chief Operator."

Sealed Orders. Boston: Houghton, Osgood, 1880. Contains "Sealed Orders," "Old Mother Goose," "The Lady of Shalott," "The True Story of Guenever," "Doherty," "The Voyage of the 'America,' " "Wrecked in Port," "Running the Risk," "Long, Long Ago," "Since I Died," "A Woman's Pulpit," "Number 13," "Two Hundred and Two," "Cloth of Gold," "Saint Caligula," "Miss Mildred's Friend," "Neblitt."

6. Uncollected magazine fiction

"Comrades." *Harper's New Monthly* 123 (Aug., 1911):398-406. Also published individually, New York: Harper, 1911.

"An Hour with Gwendolyn [Harleth of Eliot's *Danial Deronda*]." *Sunday Afternoon* 3 (Mar., 1879):230-34.

"Jonathan and David." *Harper's New Monthly* 109 (Aug., 1904):364-73. Also published individually, New York: Harper, 1909.

"Loveliness: A Story." *Atlantic Monthly* 84 (Aug., 1899):216-29. Also published individually, Boston and New York: Houghton, Mifflin, 1899.

"Margaret Bronson." *Harper's New Monthly* 31 (Sept., 1865):498-504.

"A Sacrifice Consumed." *Harper's New Monthly* 28 (Jan., 1864):235-40.

"The Supply at St. Agatha's." *Century* 25 (Apr., 1894):868-76. Also published individually, Boston and New York: Houghton, Mifflin, 1896.

"Zerviah Hope." *Scribner's* 21 (Nov., 1880):78-88. Also in *Stories by American Authors,* Vol. 7 (New York: Scribner's, 1884).

7. Verse

Poetic Studies. Boston: James R. Osgood, 1875.

Songs of the Silent World and Other Poems. Boston and New York: Houghton, Mifflin, 1884. Includes "The Sphinx," "Victurae Salutamus."

8. Drama

Within the Gates. Boston and New York: Houghton, Mifflin, 1901. Also *McClure's* 17 (May-July, 1901):35-43, 142-49, 236-50.

9. Work co-authored with Herbert Dickinson Ward

Come Forth. Boston and New York: Houghton, Mifflin, 1891.

A Lost Hero. Boston: Roberts, 1891. (Juvenile)

The Master of the Magicians. Boston and New York: Houghton, Mifflin, 1890.

"The Secretary's Murderer." *Harper's Bazar* 24 (Jan. 31, 1891):83.

10. Major collections of unpublished materials, esp. correspondence

Andover Historical Society

Boston Public Library: Department of Rare Books and Manuscripts

The Essex Institute: James Duncan Phillips Library

Harvard University: The Houghton Library

The Rutherford B. Hayes Library: Mary and William Claflin Papers

The Huntington Library

The New York Public Library: Century Collection and Elizabeth Garver Jordan Papers, Manuscripts and Archives Division, Astor, Lenox and Tilden Foundations

Radcliffe College: The Arthur and Elizabeth Schlesinger Library on the
    History of Women in America
Swarthmore College: Friends Historical Library
University of Virginia: Clifton Waller Barrett Collection, Manuscripts
    Department, Alderman Library
Yale University: The Beinecke Rare Book and Manuscript Library

SECONDARY SOURCES

1. Books, parts of books, and articles

Bennett, Mary Angela. *Elizabeth Stuart Phelps.* Philadelphia:
    University of Pennsylvania Press, 1939. The only previous
    book-length study, a factual literary biography covering all
    phases of the published work. Exhaustive bibliography (pp.
    139-59), excluding *Woman's Journal* contributions; indi-
    cates serial appearances of collected short works.

Douglas [Wood], Ann. "'Fashionable Diseases': Women's
    Complaints and their Treatment in Nineteenth-Century
    America." *Journal of Interdisciplinary History* 4 (1973):
    25-52. Cites *Doctor Zay* as an example of role reversal
    suggestive of the power struggle implicit in physician-
    patient relations.

Habegger, Alfred. "Nineteenth-Century American Humor:
    Easy-going Males, Anxious Ladies, and Penelope Lapham."
    PMLA 91 (Oct., 1976):891-99. Cites Mrs. Butterwell of
    Doctor Zay as an example of feminist humor.

Kessler, Carol Farley. "The Feminist Mock-Heroics of Elizabeth
    Stuart Phelps." *Regionalism and the Female Imagination* 3
    (Fall, 1977):20-28. Discusses *Old Maid's Paradise* and
    Burglars in Paradise as humorous expositions of the ways of
    man to woman; amplifies chap. 3 here.

_____. "A Literary Legacy: Elizabeth Stuart Phelps, Mother
    and Daughter." *Frontiers: A Journal of Women Studies* 5,
    no. 3 (Fall, 1980):28-33. Examines the influence of the
    mother's fiction and life upon the daughter's *Story of Avis;*
    amplifies chaps. 1 and 4 here.

_____. "Reservations: Women versus Marriage in Novels by Elizabeth Stuart Phelps (1844-1911)." *Proceedings for the National Convention of the Popular Culture Association.* Bowling Green, Ohio: Bowling Green State University Press, 1976, pp. 1148-52. Considers depiction of marriage in *Silent Partner, Avis, Friends,* and *A Singular Life.* Amplified in chaps. 3 and 4 here.

St. Armand, Barton Levi. "Heaven Deferred: The Image of Heaven in the Works of Emily Dickinson and Elizabeth Stuart Phelps." *American Quarterly* 29 (1977):55-78. Finds the heavenly imagery of *The Gates Ajar* a gloss for Dickinson's poetry.

Smith, Helen Sootin, ed. Introduction to *The Gates Ajar.* The John Harvard Library. Cambridge: Belknap Press, Harvard University Press, 1964, pp. v-xxxiii. An essential psycho-literary analysis of the book, its literary and biographical backgrounds, as well as a close textual reading.

Spring, Rebecca T. "Elizabeth Stuart Phelps." In *Our Famous Women.* Hartford, Conn.: A. D. Worthington, 1883, pp. 560-79. A biographical sketch of Phelps's early life, concluding at mid-career. Anecdotal; contemporary response to fiction through 1882.

Stansell, Christine. "Elizabeth Stuart Phelps: A Study in Rebellion." *Massachusetts Review* 13 (1972): 239-56. Important early examination of Phelps's *Gates Ajar, Avis, Old Maid's Paradise, Doctor Zay,* within the context of her life and work.

Stewart, G[race] B. "Mother, Daughter, and the Birth of the Female Artist." *Women's Studies* 6 (Nov., 1978): 127-46. (Expanded as chap. 4 of *A New Mythos: The Novel of the Artist as Heroine 1877-1977,* St. Alban's, Vt.: Eden Press, 1979). Mentions *The Story of Avis* as it exemplifies the Demeter/Persephone myth.

Ward, Susan. "The Career Woman Fiction of E. S. Phelps," Proceedings of the Nineteenth Century Women Writers' Conference, *Hofstra University Cultural and International Studies.* New York: AMS, forthcoming. Discusses Phelps's feminist views and how they influenced both the content and form of her career fiction.

Welter, Barbara. "Defenders of the Faith." In *Dimity Convictions: The American Woman in the Nineteeth Century.* Athens: Ohio University Press, 1976, pp. 111-20. Considers Phelps beside Augusta Evans Wilson and Margaret Deland as writers seeking to perpetuate a religious view of life.

2. Unpublished dissertations

Coultrap-McQuin, Susan Margaret. "Elizabeth Stuart Phelps: The Cultural Context of a Nineteenth-Century Professional Writer." Ph. D. dissertation, University of Iowa, 1979. Sociological emphasis complements Kessler's emphasis. Especially useful is chapter 3 on the relationship between Phelps and publishers.

Kelly, Lori Duin. " 'Oh the Poor Women!': A Study of the Works of Elizabeth Stuart Phelps." Ph. D. dissertation, University of North Carolina, 1979. Surveys the life and work with chapters on Phelps's religious and feminist writing and on her nontraditional female characters and fictional critiques of marriage. Published as *The Life and Works of Elizabeth Stuart Phelps, Victorian Feminist Writer.* Troy, New York: Whitston Publishing Company, 1982.

Kessler, Carol Farley. " 'The Woman's Hour': Life and Novels of Elizabeth Stuart Phelps, 1844-1911." Ph. D. dissertation, University of Pennsylvania, 1977. Places the living and writing within a social and historical context.

Index